The Imitation of
Nature

The Imitation of Nature

John Hyman

Basil Blackwell

Copyright © John Hyman 1989

First published 1989

Basil Blackwell Ltd
108 Cowley Road, Oxford, OX4 1JF, UK

Basil Blackwell Inc.
432 Park Avenue South, Suite 1503
New York, NY 10016, USA

British Library Cataloguing in Publication Data

A CIP catalogue record for this book is available
from the British Library.

Library of Congress Cataloging in Publication Data

Hyman, John.
The imitation of nature.
Bibliography: p.
Includes index.
1. Art—Philosophy.   I. Title.
N71.H96 1989   700'.1   88–7679

ISBN 0–631–16373–5

Typeset in 11 on 13pt Caslon Old Face
by Hope Services, Abingdon
Printed in Great Britain by
T. J. Press Ltd, Padstow

To the memory of my mother
Aimer purement, c'est consentir à la distance

Contents

Acknowledgements for Plates and Figures

The author and publisher are grateful to the following for their kind permission to reproduce plates: Alinari, Florence 6, 7, 13, 29; Byzantine Visual Resources, © 1988, Dumbarton Oaks, Washington, DC 14; Peter Clayton 28; Deutsches Archäologisches Institut, Athens 21; after Diehl, Le Tourneau, Saladin 12; Mansell Collection 2, 9, 18; Martin von Wagner–Museum der Universität Würzburg (Photograph: K. Öhrlein) 5; The Metropolitan Museum of Art, Fletcher Fund, 1932 (32.11.1), All Rights Reserved 20; National Gallery, London 8, 11; Società Scala, Florence 1; Staatliche Antiken-sammlungen und Glypothek München 15; Drawings by Steinberg; © 1955, 1983 The New Yorker Magazine, Inc. 16; Tapisserie de Bayeux with special permission from the City of Bayeux 24, 25, 26, 27; The Trustees of the British Museum 3, 4, 17, 19, 22, 23.

We also wish to thank the following for their kind permission to reproduce figures: Ashmolean Library, Oxford fig. 6; Verlag Ploetz GmbH & Co KG, Freiburg fig. 5.

List of Illustrations

Figures

Plates between pages 46 and 47

Preface

No student of ancient visual theory who is alert to the distinction between factual and conceptual investigations will fail to notice that the first efforts to explain the phenomenon of sight were stimulated by conceptual confusion, and not only by puzzlement or curiosity about the causes of empirical facts.

The capacity to learn about the perceptible environment was not *per se* of interest to ancient philosopher-scientists; it was the capacity to learn about the world *apparently without coming into contact with it* that puzzled them. However, the question that lay at the heart of ancient visual theory was not how it is possible to learn about the world without contact, which is what the sighted ostensibly do. For their speculation about the sense of sight was always constrained by the principle that perception without contact is *impossible* (v. Aristotle, *De Sensu*, 4.422ª29). Philosophers therefore postulated a sort of *ersatz* contact between the visible object and the perceiving subject, and disagreed over what sort of contact this was.

This might seem to be a perfectly sensible way to conduct an empirical investigation of the sense of sight. First advance the working hypothesis that perception without contact is impossible, and hence that vision is possible only by virtue of a particular sort of contact between the visible object and the perceiving subject that is itself imperceptible to the unaided senses; and then try to identify what sort of contact this is. But this procedure presupposes an explanation of the fact that certain sorts of contact do enable us to perceive. In other words, if it is an empircal hypothesis that perception without contact is not possible, then it is an empirical question, why perception *with* contact *is* possible. But the ancient philosophers who adopted the principle that perception without contact is impossible did not even pose this question.

This was not an oversight. For the principle that perception without contact is impossible was not an empirical hypothesis at all; it was the reflection of a pervasive source of philosophical perplexity, the power exerted by a conceptual paradigm. Because the name of a substance is the paradigm case of a substantive, philosophers seek to identify special objects to correspond to the substantive expressions that deviate from the paradigm – numerals, for example. In a similar way, tactile perception was regarded as the paradigm case of perception, and therefore received little attention from ancient philosophers; and it was principally the deviation from this paradigm that theorists of vision sought to explain. Physical contact is a logically necessary condition for tactile perception, except for the perception of heat and cold: without contact, it is (logically) impossible to feel, for example, the shape of a coin. But the visual perception of shape is not constrained in this way. Philosophers therefore sought to identify the go-between which, so it seemed, was needed in order to mediate between the visible object and the perceiving subject.

One popular candidate for the role of go-between was a picture. Just as an image in a pool of water allows us to see whatever is reflected in it, so, it was thought, the image of the visible environment of a person that is plainly present in his eye (in fact, the image reflected by the cornea) allows him to see what it depicts. This image was perfectly suited to its task: a picture enables us to discern the visible features of whatever it depicts; this particular picture is in contact with the perceiving subject – indeed with the organ of sight – and depicts what he sees. It is no longer difficult to show that this argument is fallacious. A picture cannot possibly play the role in which it is cast here, for we discern what a picture depicts by looking at it. Hence it must be presented to the eye in the same manner as any other feature of the visible environment; and so it cannot be the thing that does the presenting.

In fact, the pictorial emanation postulated by the ancients was a candidate for a mythological office, for nothing is needed to present the visible features of an object to the eye, in the manner of a simulacrum: contact with the eye, far from permitting vision, generally precludes it. Moreover, the suggestion that a pictorial emanation conveys to the eye the visible features of whatever it depicts (and proceeds from) already evinces the failure to distinguish between a go-between and a surrogate. This failure is one of the chief sources of error in visual theory, but it is also a highly important issue in the philosophical study of depiction for independent reasons. For example, the Iconoclast controversy in the eighth-century Byzantine empire, during which philosophical debate concerning depiction assumed a cultural and political significance far greater than it enjoys nowadays, was concerned precisely with the failure to distinguish between a go-between and a surrogate, in respect of devotional images. For although the arguments of the opposing camps were mostly theological – was the depiction of Christ possible given His two natures?[1] – the fundamental claim of the iconoclasts was that devotional imagery is idolatrous because an icon is a surrogate object of worship, and the fundamental claim of the iconodules was that an icon, like a go-between, conveys the worshipper's devotion to the person depicted.

The *a priori* visual theory that I have described was certainly confused, but it was not ineffectual, for it provided the guiding analogy of visual theory in the modern age. The ancient philosophers who argued that we see by means of an image compared the exercise of the faculty of sight with the performance of a particular visual task – identifying what is depicted in a picture. It may seem futile to explain visual perception in terms of the performance of a particular visual task, and I shall argue that a great deal of confusion has been generated by precisely this feature of the analogy. Nevertheless, the pictorial analogy, variously transmuted, has dominated the study of vision ever since Alhazen succeeded in combining it with the mathematical theory of vision. One consequence of the power that it has exerted on the imagination of visual theorists was a muddle that was regarded for eight hundred years as 'the principal point in the whole optic theory' (Berkeley). This, in the form that it has taken since the beginning of the seventeenth century, is the problem of the inversion and reversal of

---

[1] The argument, expounded at the Trullan Council, that opposition to the portrayal of Christ in human form was inconsistent with the doctrine of the Incarnation was ingeniously countered by extending the Christological disputes of earlier centuries: the portrayal of Christ, it was claimed, presumed either that His two natures were separate (the Nestorian heresy), or else that they were mixed (the Monophysite heresy).

the retinal image. How, it was asked, can we see the world upright in spite of the inversion of the retinal image? The question is no longer asked; it has, so to speak, gone cold. Nevertheless, it is subjected to scrutiny in this essay in the hope that rather as painters once learned anatomy from the dissection of corpses, the study of a dead philosphical problem will teach lessons about its living relatives.

A major part of the philosopher's business is to disentangle conceptual puzzles that have been woven into the fabric of empirical research. Empirical problems are not *per se* the philosopher's concern; and the importance of a philosophical enterprise of this sort can be judged by the extent to which the coherence of the scientific project depends upon these threads of conceptual confusion. If one sees the history of science as the story of an inexorable drive forward, the paradigm of intellectual progress – as it is popularly seen today – then one will expect the philosopher to find little work to do. But the evidence examined in the first and third chapters of this essay suggests that at least as far as the history of visual theory is concerned, this is a false picture. The history of visual theory is of course a history of progress. Nobody before Kepler was able to describe the optics of the eye correctly. But it is also, and no less, a history of the accumulation of error. Indeed the great steps forward, Alhazen's and Kepler's, went hand in hand with the multiplication of error and confusion, for

> . . . ere a man hath power to say 'Behold!'
> The jaws of darkness do devour it up:
> So quick bright things come to confusion.

Identifying what is depicted in a picture is a visual task. Consequently, philosophers, psychologists and art historians who have sought to explain the nature of depiction in general and the nature of particular pictorial techniques have drawn heavily on whatever visual theory was available to them. The chief purpose of this essay is to examine the influence of visual theory on the history and theory of art, particularly in respect of the origins of naturalism in ancient art, and the development of the system of artificial perspective in fifteenth-century Florence. It is generally acknowledged that Greek painting in the fifth century BC saw a decisive shift away from the formulaic, and that the depiction of spatial relations was profoundly changed by the invention of the system of artificial perspective. This essay is concerned with the explanation of these changes, and the visual theory that has influenced the historiography of art in these areas.

It follows that although this is an essay in aesthetics, many questions which have loomed large in the recent literature in aesthetics will not be touched on. There is, for example, no discussion whatever of the various attempts that have been made to deploy in the discussion of the visual arts concepts that belong principally to the analysis of language. In particular, the chapter which deals with the system of artificial perspective (chapter 4) does not address the question whether the relationship between a perspective painting and the scene it depicts is a *natural* relationship (like the relationship between a daughter and her mother) or a *conventional* one (like the relationship between a daughter-in-law and her mother-in-law). Frankly, I doubt whether mooting these alternatives is the best way to characterize the achievement of the inventors and first exponents of the system of artificial perspective, I doubt whether the function of the system is to establish a relationship of any particular sort between pictures and what they depict, and I doubt whether there is a non-trivial sense in which perspective paintings of the Taj Mahal, the retreat from Moscow, and the Last Judgment stand in the same relationship, or a relationship of the same sort, to what they respectively depict. Be that as it may, the conventionalist thesis and the debate it has provoked are simply outside the compass of this essay.[2]

As well as questions that are not broached, there are tasks that are not undertaken. Readers hoping to find a theory of vision or an 'account' of naturalism will be disappointed: theories I take to be the business of scientists, and accounts, presumably, are the business of accountants. Since the theories of vision and of naturalism that are examined in this essay are all found wanting for one reason or another, it may be thought that the author's failure to provide any alternatives to these theories is a defect in his work. To this there are two answers. First, as Nietzsche remarked, it is not necessary to build new idols in order to show that the old ones have feet of clay. Second, these theories are examined only insofar as they have contributed to, or form an indispensable part of the background to the confusion which surrounds

---

[2] It may be that the discussion of perspective that appears here has a bearing on the debate between advocates of a natural relationship and their conventionalist adversaries: I hope to examine this matter in another forum.

the questions of the origins of naturalistic painting, and the development of artificial perspective. Their merits and demerits are assessed only for this purpose.[3] Inevitably, I am led to consider in what sense a picture can be said to reproduce the appearance of what it depicts; and I am compelled to investigate the relationship between the concept of vision and the concept of visual experience. These problems, of course, are fundamental ones: theorists of depiction and of vision must address them, and their theories are judged in no small part by the cogency of the solutions they offer. Nevertheless, my own treatment of these matters does not belong to a theoretical enterprise. On the contrary, it is part of the purpose of this essay to shed light on the nature and origins of naturalistic painting and on the achievement of the inventors of artificial perspective *without* recourse to theories of vision or of naturalism. One hopes that the method will be judged by its results.

Instead of advocating a theory of depiction or of naturalism I shall, among other things, examine Plato's hostility towards naturalistic painting, propose an explanation for the ubiquity of the profile in early near-Eastern painting and carving, and suggest how these matters are related. If this does not sound much like traditional philosophical aesthetics, so much the better. Since its inception in the eighteenth century, philosophical aesthetics has been modelled on moral philosophy. It has been dedicated to the so-called Problem of Taste, that is to the problem of the objectivity of aesthetic judgements, and to a sort of freelance anatomy of Key Aesthetic Concepts – Art, Beauty, the Sublime, Expression, and so forth. Moral philosophy has changed, but philosophical aesthetics has not; and since 1945 it has, with a few exceptions, contributed little to our understanding of art.

[3] Undoubtedly, there are more plausible, or at any rate more sophisticated and more fashionable theories of vision than those examined in this essay – most obviously, theories deriving from research in artificial intelligence and machine vision – but they have not so far influenced the way we think about the differences between Egyptian and Greek painting, or the way we explain the fact that shading and perspective diminution were invented in Athens in the lifetime of Socrates, rather than in Egypt in the lifetime of Akhenaten, or Constantinople in the lifetime of Justinian. In fact, I quote an eminent machine theorist (see pp. 71 f.), but the remark I quote is more or less independent of the author's research in machine theory, and my comments on the remark are not intended to have any bearing on the usefulness or validity of this sort of visual theory.

It is a regrettable irony that Wittgenstein's conception of philosophy as the extirpation of conceptual confusion has been seen as introverted and unambitious: a talking-cure for the treatment of philosophers by themselves. For the reverse is the truth. Philosophers do not have a monopoly on conceptual confusion and philosophical aesthetics, for example, conducted in accordance with Wittgenstein's conception of the goals, methods and parameters of philosophical enquiry, can expect to become more closely involved with the history of art and the study of literature: students of aesthetics will have to abandon the contented seclusion of their own community and the cosy, familiar problems they have studied for two centuries. But as Wittgenstein wrote,

> The philosopher is not a citizen of any community of ideas. That is what makes him into a philosopher.

Many people have commented on parts of this work. I am particularly indebted to Mr John Ashton, Professor A. Crombie, Professor R.L. Gregory, Professor A. Margalit, Dr David Ricks, Mr Bede Rundle, Professor R. Scruton and Professor L. Weiskrantz. Sir Peter Strawson gave me much friendly advice, and showed unfailing solicitude and good humour. I have benefited greatly from this privilege, and I wish to record my gratitude to him. I am also grateful to friendly and challenging audiences at Haifa University, and at the Hebrew University, Jerusalem.

My teacher and friend, Dr Peter Hacker, has read practically everything I have written on this subject. I owe him more than I can well express.

I

The Cartesian theory of vision

Metaphor and analogy are the scaffolding of science. Kepler's theory of
the retinal image could not have been built without the analogy
between an eye and a camera obscura, and, two hundred and fifty years
later, Charles Darwin devoted most of the first chapter of *The Origin of
Species* to a discussion of pigeon fanciers. Unlike Darwin, Kepler was
bewitched by his own imagination and was led to wonder 'how this
image or picture is joined to the visual faculty, which is situated in the
retina and in the [optic] nerve, and whether it is placed within the
hollows of the brain, before the soul or tribunal or the visual faculty,
or whether the visual faculty, like a magistrate sent by the soul from
the administrative chamber of the brain, descends into the optic nerve
or retina to meet this image, as though to a lower court' (Kepler, 1939,
pp. 151–2).

The theory of the retinal image answered the crucial question of
medieval optics: the scaffolding had served its purpose and should have
been dismantled. Instead, Kepler mistook it for a part of the building:
what he construed as a scientific problem was nothing more than the
extension of a metaphor. As a result, and in spite of his remarkable
achievement, he left the theory of vision in a state of confusion.

In this first chapter I shall describe Descartes' revolutionary attempt
to extirpate that confusion. I intend to show that Descartes revolutionized
visual theory by manipulating a pair of analogies which had dominated
visual theory since its inception and by advancing a theory of depiction
which has since become orthodox. Advocates of the first analogy
suggest that seeing the world is rather like seeing pictures of it;
Kepler's analogy between the eye and a camera obscura, which was

anticipated by Leonardo da Vinci, was a variation on this theme. Advocates of the second analogy compare vision to the use of a walking-stick: the air transmits an impression of a visible object to the eye rather as a walking-stick enables us to find our way around in the dark by transmitting pressures to the hand. As I shall show, Descartes' rejection of the pictorial analogy in favour of the walking-stick analogy and his theory of depiction were designed to salvage Kepler's theory of the retinal image, a pearl of great price, from its murky setting.

Descartes aimed to show that whilst Kepler's theory of the retinal image correctly described the optics of the eye, the pictorial analogy was misleading and stood in the way of a mechanistic theory of perception. Naturally, the main obstacle facing Descartes was that Kepler's theory was generally supposed to have vindicated the claims of traditional intromissionism. (Intromissionism is the theory that radiation enters the eye, and does not issue from it.) It was universally agreed, first, that Kepler had confirmed that the form or species postulated by the intromissionists was to be found on the retina, and second, that he had correctly described the manner of its transmission to and through the eye. Of course, this interpretation of Kepler's achievement in optics was likely to be well subscribed, for it was Kepler's own.

It is generally supposed that modern visual theory begins with Kepler. Alisdair Crombie, for example, suggests that Kepler successfully explained the optics of the eye because he embraced what Crombie calls 'the mechanistic hypothesis' – that is because he decided to expound a theory of vision within the constraints of a mechanistic physiology. 'Leonardo did not solve the dioptric problem of the eye,' Crombie explains, 'for reasons that are clear in all his accounts and constructions. His analysis of vision was based on Alhazen's, and for the same reason as Alhazen he found it necessary to look for a physical arrangement that would produce an image that was upright and correctly orientated left and right.' (Crombie, 1967, p. 39). 'Kepler's discovery in 1603 of the dioptric mechanism by which the eye forms an image dealt with a problem . . . intimately part of a new approach to physiology, explicitly revolutionary in its ambitions and in its consequences' (ibid., p. 3).

In fact, Kepler was baffled by the inversion and reversal of the retinal image. His struggle to avoid it and, when this had failed, his unconvincing answer to the question, why does an inverted retinal image not cause inverted vision? (see below, p. 7) are enough to cast doubt on Crombie's claim. Besides, the retina was first recognized as the sensitive ocular organ by Felix Platter (1536–1614) and the lens was first drawn in the front part of the eye at about the same time: the optics of the eye could not have been correctly explained before these discoveries were made. Be that as it may, Crombie suggests that a medieval problem had to be reformulated before it could be solved; whilst there are no absolute endings and beginnings in the history of science, it is the chief purpose of this chapter to demonstrate that Kepler solved a medieval problem and that Descartes reformulated the solution.[1]

Intromissionism was developed and defended by the atomists. Democritus (active in the second half of the fifth century BC) maintained that perception, of whatever modality, is caused by an emanation qualitatively like the perceptual object from which it comes. In the case of vision this thin film of atoms, compared by Lucretius to the skin of a snake,[2] bears the *visible* properties of the object – its form and colour – rather than its smell, sound or taste. Since vision, of all the senses, absorbed the attention of philosophers, what Democritus called a likeness (*deikelōn*) was soon called an image (*eidōlōn*). Theophrastus, Aristotle's successor at the Lyceum, wrote that 'the majority hold that vision is the result of an image being in the eye': the image to which he was referring was certainly the image visible on the cornea.[3]

---

[1] Descartes also corrected Kepler's theory of the retinal image: he treated the lens in its actual lenticular shape, whereas Kepler had treated it as a sphere. Furthermore, he correctly attributed accommodation to changes in the shape of the lens, rather than its position.

[2] Lucretius writes that 'amongst visible things many throw off bodies, sometimes loosely diffused abroad as wood throws off smoke and fire heat; sometimes more close-knit and condensed, as often when cicadas drop their thin coats in summer, and when calves at birth throw off the caul from their outermost surface, and also when the slippery serpent casts off his vesture among the thorns; . . . since these things happen, a thin image must also be thrown off from things, from the outermost surface of things.' (Lucretius, *De Rerum Natura*, IV, 54–64)

[3] The Greek *korē*, as meaning 'pupil', is etymologically derived from the use of the same word to mean 'girl' or 'puppet'. In fact, the Greeks took the corneal reflection to

Thus ancient intromissionism answered the question of what form of contact between observer and object permits vision by postulating a contact mediated by the image of the visible object. This analogy between straightforward visual perception and the indirect visual perception of an object mediated by its mirror image, or by an artificial reproduction of its appearance, served, paradoxically, both to explain vision and to express scepticism with regard to the power of the senses: Sextus Empiricus records that 'Anaxarchus and Monimus likened existing things to a scene painting, and supposed them to resemble the impressions experienced in sleep and madness.'

Extramissionism – the theory that radiation issues from the eye – was proposed by Euclid, and developed by Ptolemy. However, Euclid's theory of vision was not meant to be assessed by physical criteria (although Ptolemy tried to supply the serious physical content that it lacked); it was a mathematical theory, intended to provide a geometrical definition of the visual field. (See below, chapter 4.)

The physical alternative to intromissionism was a mediumistic optical theory, according to which vision occurs as a result of qualitative changes in the air or transparent medium between the eye and the perceptual object. Whilst Plato and Aristotle defended (very different) versions of this theory, its guiding analogy was provided by the Stoics who, as Galen records, 'say that we see by means of the surrounding air as with a walking-stick': the cone of air between the eye and the perceptual object is stamped at its base with an impression of the object, and this is instantaneously transmitted to the eye, just as a walking-stick transmits pressures to the hand.

Mathematics aside, these two powerful analogies were the most enduring fruit of ancient visual theory; but the theory of vision did not begin to assume its modern form until the eleventh century.

The first serious student of optics in the Islamic world, al-Kindi (d. *c*.866), was an extramissionist. al-Kindi rejected intromissionism – which, so he believed, contaminated all visual theories except the Euclidean – because it attached no importance to the spatial orientation of the visible object, with respect to the observer. The intromissionist form was conceived as an integral likeness representing the entire

be an image in the crystalline humour. For a detailed study of ancient theories of vision, v. Beare, 1906, pp. 1–92.

visible object and not merely the surface facing the observer, and so a theory of vision postulating the radiation of such forms was bound, so al-Kindi thought, to fail to provide any explanation of the different *aspects* of, say, a head seen in profile and full-face. In short, intromissionism did not appear to accommodate the laws of perspective.

Whether or not the objection is decisive – neither Plato nor Aristotle considers such an objection, which is no surprise, since their theories of vision were never meant to be judged by mathematical criteria – Alhazen (*c*.965–1039) devised an intromission theory which met it, and which constitutes the greatest medieval contribution to visual theory. Alhazen's theory incorporates a different conception of radiation into the eye, a conception which was based on the principle that 'from each point of every coloured body, illuminated by any light, issue light and colour along every straight line that can be drawn from that point'.[4] The obstacle to renouncing the notion of coherent radiation – the radiation of integral forms – which was however vulnerable to al-Kindi's objection, was that if every point on the surface of the visible object radiates in all directions, then every point in the eye should be affected by light and colour from virtually all of the visual field, and the outcome should be total confusion. In other words, how can incoherent radiation, as opposed to the radiation of integral forms, yield coherent vision?

The problem is simply that there are too many rays, for coherent vision requires that each point on the surface of the glacial humour (which Alhazen believed to be the sensitive ocular organ) receives a ray from only one point in the visual field. In other words, there must be a one-to-one correspondence between points in the visual field and points in the eye. Alhazen satisfied this requirement by dismissing as impotent every ray from a given point except the one falling perpendicular to the surface of the eye. An arrow fired directly at a target will penetrate more deeply than one which hits it at an oblique angle: similarly, the greater force of the perpendicular ray is needed to stimulate the visual power. These perpendicular rays form a pyramid or cone, whose apex is at the centre of the eye and whose base is at the surface of the objects seen.

---

[4] Alhazen's punctiform analysis of the *visible* object was directly based on al-Kindi's punctiform analysis of the *luminous* object. For a detailed exposition of Alhazen's visual theory, v. Lindberg, 1976, ch. 4.

In this way Alhazen, who appears to have been the first person to make a study of refraction by curved surfaces, imposed a geometrical–optical model on the anatomy and physiology of the eye and paved the way for Kepler's successful use of the analogy between the eye and an image-making machine. Ancient optics was divided into three relatively independent traditions: Alhazen combined the mathematical, physical and medical approaches to the study of vision into a single comprehensive theory. By the ingenious expedient of fragmenting the image of the visible object and then reassembling it in the eye, he devised an intromission scheme, based on the punctiform analysis of the visible object and the requirement of a one-to-one correspondence of points in the visual field to points in the eye, which provided the basic framework of visual theory that has prevailed until the present.

The perpendicular rays, which are responsible for vision, enter the eye without refraction and proceed towards its centre:

> However, the form cannot extend from the surface of the glacialis to the cavity of the nerve in straight lines and at the same time preserve the proper position of its parts. For all these lines converge at the centre of the eye, and once they have been extended in a straight line, their positions beyond the centre will be reversed: what is right will become left and vice versa, and what is above will become below and below above. (Alhazen, 1572, bk 2, ch. 1, s. 2)

The perpendicular rays cannot reach the centre of the eye, for if they did they would be reduced to a point and the order of the visible body would be lost; or if they continued beyond it this order would be inverted and reversed. Alhazen's intromission scheme takes account of this difficulty and ensures the refraction of the rays before they have reached the centre of the eye (v. Lindberg 1975, ch. 4). Obviously, the difficulty could not have arisen until Alhazen had fused intromissionism and the mathematical theory of vision and so he was the first visual theorist to consider the problem of the inversion and reversal of the species – a problem which was destined to become, in George Berkeley's words, 'the principal point in the whole optic theory' (Berkeley, 1975, p. 52).

The problem of one-to-one correspondence was solved, after many attempts had been thwarted by the *a priori* exclusion of a solution which resulted in an inverted and reversed image, by Johannes Kepler; but the answer was at first unwelcome. 'Indeed, I tortured myself for a long time' wrote Kepler, 'in order to show that the cones intersecting when they pass through the aperture of the uvea intersect again behind the crystalline humour in the middle of the vitreous humour, so that another inversion is produced before they reach the retina.' (1939, p. 185). The second intersection was not forthcoming, and so Kepler was compelled to offer the first in a long series of answers to the question, why an inverted image does not lead to inverted vision. Kepler's answer was as follows:

> If you are bothered by the inversion of this picture and fear that this inversion might be followed by inverted vision, I ask you to consider the following. Vision is not an action [*actio*], simply because illumination is an action, but is a sensation [*passio*], i.e. the opposite of action: hence it is fitting that the things which are acted upon [*patientia*, i.e. retinal pictures] should be placed opposite to the things that are acting upon them, so that the positions may correspond. Now the positions are perfectly opposite when all the lines connecting opposite points run through the same centre, which would not have been so if the picture had been erect. . . . Therefore, when the picture is inverted, the absurdity from which Witelo ran away does not occur . . . (Kepler, 1939, p. 185)

There is little to say about this solution. It is futile and ad hoc, and serves only to betray Kepler's incomprehension.

Kepler's conception of the eye as an image-*making* machine marks a break with the traditional intromissionist conception of the eye as an organ for *receiving* images. Nevertheless, Kepler answered the question of what form of contact between the observer and the perceptual object permits vision just as intromissionists had always answered it: he postulated a connexion which was mediated by an image of the visible object. Whilst Kepler appealed in this way to the ancient analogy between straightforward vision and the indirect visual apprehension which is mediated by a mirror image or a picture of the perceptual object, Descartes turned to the Stoic analogy:

> No doubt you have had occasion to walk at night without a light, over rough ground, and have needed a stick to guide yourself.

You may then have been able to notice that by means of this stick you could feel the various objects around you, and even discern whether they were trees or stones or sand or water or grass or mud or some other such thing. It is true that this kind of sensation, for those who do not have long experience of it, is a little confused and obscure; but consider it in those who, having been born blind, have used it all their lives . . . I want you to think of the light in bodies we call 'luminous' as no more than a certain movement, or very rapid and lively action, which passes to our eyes through the medium of the air and other transparent bodies, just as the movement or resistance of the bodies encountered by the blind man passes to his hand through the medium of his stick. (Descartes, 1953, pp. 181–2)

The use of this analogy allowed Descartes to dispense entirely with the species of intromissionists, which he referred to as 'these little images whizzing through the air . . . which so tax the imagination of philosophers' (Descartes, 1953, p. 183). Just as nothing travels to the blind man through his stick, no form or species enters the eye of the sighted. Descartes has several objections to the traditional notion of the species. To begin with, he doubts whether such things could be formed by the objects of vision and wonders how they could be received by the eyes and transmitted to the brain. He suggests, furthermore, that their advocates have ignored that the mind can be stimulated by signs and by words which, unlike pictures, do not resemble what they represent. And besides, no picture can resemble its prototype entirely; otherwise, it would not be a picture, but the thing itself. I shall shortly examine this last objection in greater detail.

The argument which today is widely considered to be a definitive answer to the problem of the inversion and reversal of the retinal image began life as a further and almost parenthetical objection to the traditional notion of the species. Having explained Kepler's theory of the retinal image in the fifth discourse of the *Dioptrique*, 'Concerning the Images which are formed on the Back of the Eye', Descartes begins the sixth, 'Concerning Vision', as follows:

Now, this picture, which travels in this way to the inside of our head, still bears some resemblance to the things from which it proceeds. However, as I have already explained at sufficient length, one must not suppose that it is by means of this resemblance that it makes us aware of them, as if there were yet another pair of eyes in our heads with which we could see it; rather, it is the movements of which it is constituted, which, acting immediately on the soul, inasmuch as it is united to the body, are ordained by nature to make it have such sensations. (Descartes, 1953, p. 217)

This argument is not as straightforward as it appears to be, for Descartes exploits the time-honoured equivocation over whether the species is presented to the soul for inspection, in the spirit of the traditional intromissionist analogy, or whether, as an Aristotelian form, it is in the soul (*De Anima*, $431^b30-432^a1$)[5], in order to thrust upon a reader the abrupt choice between embracing the absurdity that the soul has eyes and allowing that our ideas need not resemble their causes. The intromissionist species is ridiculed, but the Aristotelian form is Descartes' real target. Be that as it may, Descartes cannot countenance traditional intromissionism because the distinction between primary and secondary qualities, essential to Cartesian as to Galilean science, is incompatible with the traditional conception of the species, which 'requires only that they bear a resemblance to the objects they represent' (Descartes, 1953, p. 203). By contrast, the Stoic analogy was easily accommodated within a ruthlessly mechanistic physiology and enabled Descartes to incorporate Kepler's theory of the retinal image into a comprehensive theory of perception whose independent explanations of the perception of primary and secondary qualities avoided the implication that nature is not fully intelligible in mathematical terms.[6]

As far as the perception of light and colour are concerned, the message is unequivocal:

[5] This equivocation finds an echo in the later use of the camera obscura as an analogy both for the eye and for the perceiving subject. For example, Locke writes as follows: '. . . . methinks the understanding is not much unlike a closet wholly shut from light, with only some little opening left, to let in external visible resemblances, or ideas of things without' (Locke, 1961, II, xi, 17. V. Yolton, 1984, ch. VII).

[6] I use the terms 'primary qualities' and 'secondary qualities' for convenience, although Descartes did not use them.

. . . we must believe that our soul is of such a nature, that the force of the movements in the regions of the brain where the optic-fibres originate makes it have the sensation of brightness; and the manner of these movements give it the sensation of colour.[7] (1953, p. 217)

But when Descartes considers the visual perception of primary qualities his aims are different. Primary qualities are not, unlike colour, light and pain, mere sensations. We are wrong to attribute colour to bodies, just as we are wrong to locate a toothache in a tooth; but 'we can observe in these same objects many other features, such as size, shape, number, and so forth, which exist in them just as our sense, or rather our understanding, makes us perceive them' (*Principes*, p. 606).

A task which is an essential preliminary to Descartes' treatment of the visual perception of primary qualities is accomplished at the end of the fourth discourse. As I have already said, he objects to the traditional notion of the species that no picture can resemble its prototype entirely; otherwise it would not be a picture, but the thing itself. Carefully restricting the discussion to engravings, which lack colour, he continues as follows:

An image need only resemble its object in a few respects; indeed, the perfection of an image often requires that it resemble its object less than it might. This is evident in the case of engravings, where a little ink placed here and there on a piece of paper makes us think of [*nous representent*] forests, towns, men, and even battles and tempests, even though, of the innumerable different qualities in these objects that they recall, they resemble

---

[7] It is an indication of Descartes' intellectual agility that he defends this crucial claim with arguments which were traditionally employed to defend both intromissionism and extramissionism. 'It seems to someone who has been struck in the eye,' he writes, 'that he can see innumerable sparks and flashes in front of him, even if his eyes are closed, or he is in a very dark place; hence this sensation must be attributed to the force of the blow, which stimulates the optic nerve-fibres as a bright light would' (1953, pp. 217–18). This had been taken as a sign of 'intraocular fire', and hence an argument for extramissionism. Descartes then suggests that his view is confirmed by the existence of after-images, which Alhazen had considered to be an argument against extramissionism.

them only in shape. And even this resemblance is very imperfect, since engravings represent bodies of varying relief and depth on a surface which is entirely flat. Moreover, in accordance with the rules of perspective, circles are often better represented by ovals than by other circles; squares by rhombuses rather than by other squares, and so on for all other shapes. And thus, so that they should be more perfect as images, and represent objects better, they must not resemble them. Now we must think of the images formed in our brain in just the same way . . . (p. 204)

This passage has been construed as a slackening in Descartes' obdurate repudiation of the pictorial analogy. (V. Gaukroger, 1980, p. 29.) Not a bit of it! Its purpose is to sanitize thoroughly the notion of a picture, so that he can begin the following discourse by admitting that 'the object we look at do imprint more or less perfect images on the back of our eyes' (Descartes, 1953, p. 205). If his readership is not to fall again into the very errors he has just laboured to extirpate, he must demonstrate that Kepler's theory does not support the claims of traditional intromissionism, as Kepler himself supposed. The passage reproduced above is devoted to that purpose.

Descartes' solution is to propose a causal theory of depiction: the success of a picture depends upon its propensity to cause an observer to enjoy the visual experience which would be occasioned by what it depicts. Similarly, the retinal picture and the 'images formed in our brain' (i.e. the patterns on the pineal gland which are caused by the retinal picture) are simply patterns of stimulation which cause the sensations of light and colour and, when treated with sufficient care, allow us to discern the extension, figure, etc. of material bodies.

The problem is simply to know how they can enable the soul to be aware of [*sentir*] all the various qualities of the objects to which they correspond, and not in the least to know how they can bear a resemblance to these objects. (Descartes, 1953, p. 204)

This theory of depiction and the theory of perception on which it depends will be examined in the next chapter. For the moment, I shall confine myself to the observation that although Descartes devised it specifically in order to mechanize the retinal image, the causal theory of depiction now enjoys enormous popularity amongst scientists, philosophers and art historians. It is succinctly advanced by Gombrich as follows:

> What may make a painting like a distant view through a window is not the fact that the two can be as indistinguishable as is a facsimile from the original: it is the similarity between the mental activities both can arouse . . . (Gombrich, 1973, p. 240)[8]

By thus treating pictures in general and retinal pictures in particular as mere patterns of sensory stimulation, Descartes can regard them in the same light as any other physiological effects of the objects of vision. Our senses are prone to deceive us about the size and shape, etc. of visible objects, and our dependence upon them must be balanced by the surer authority of reason:

> I find in myself two very different ideas of the sun: in virtue of one, which derives from the senses, . . . the sun appears to me to be very small; in the virtue of the other, derived from the reasoning of astronomy, in other words from certain notions innate in me, . . . it seems to me to be several times larger than the earth. Certainly, these two ideas of the sun cannot both resemble the same sun; and reason makes me believe that the one that derives directly from its appearance is the one that resembles it least. (Descartes, *Meditations*, pp. 288–9)

Nevertheless, the various stimuli which are caused by visible objects and which include the changes in the brain that result from changes in

---

[8] M.H. Pirenne advances the same claim as follows: 'The painting is an *object*, which does produce visual percepts in the observers . . . which resemble those which would be given by the (actual or imaginary) scene represented' (Pirenne, 1970, p. 10).

The close link between the causal theory of depiction and the causal theory of perception is explicit in Wollheim's exposition: 'By straightforward perception I mean the capacity that we humans and other animals have of perceiving things present to the senses. Any single exercise of this capacity is probably best explained in terms of the occurrence of an appropriate perceptual experience and the correct causal link between the experience and the thing or things perceived. . . . [The ability to discern what is depicted in a picture] derives from a special perceptual capacity, which presupposes, but is something over and above, straightforward perception. This special perceptual capacity is something which some animals may share but almost certainly most don't, and it allows us to have perceptual experiences of things that are not present to the senses . . .' (Wollheim, 1980, p. 217)

the shape of the lens,[1] and changes in the orientation of the head or the eyes as well as the pineal patterns caused by retinal stimulation, can, as it were, be weighed and sifted in the light of our knowledge of the world in general and our innate mastery of the *a priori* science of geometry in particular, and may thus enable us to judge correctly the extension, figure, etc. of visible things.

The visual perception of primary qualities is considered in the *Dioptrique* under four headings, namely '*la situation*', '*la distance*', '*la grandeur*', '*la figure*'. Only the translation of the first of these terms presents any difficulty; the others mean, respectively, 'distance', 'size', and 'shape'. But '*la situation*' means both 'position' and 'bearing', and should therefore be understood as position in a specifically directional sense. In other words, the *situation* of an object or a part of one is naturally identified by means of a deictic gesture, by pointing, and not by means of a description, and so the visual perception of *situation* is perfectly attuned to the walking-stick analogy. As Descartes explains: 'As regards position, i.e. the side to which each part of the object lies, with respect to our body, we perceive it by means of our eyes just as we do by means of our hands.' (1953, p. 220)

I have laboured this detail of translation because it reveals that this part of the *Dioptrique* is based on a punctiform analysis of the visible object. The table at which I am seated does not lie in a specific direction from my body or from my eyes, but each point on its surface, considered separately, does. Descartes considers any object of vision as an array of visible points, each of which lies in a given direction and at a given distance from the observer and is seen independently of all the others.

Of course, Descartes' punctiform analysis of the visible object is quite unlike its ancestor, Alhazen's; for Descartes rejects intromissionism altogether, in favour of a mediumistic theory of light adapted from Aristotle and well suited to the walking-stick analogy.[9] Each point on

---

[9] 'There is no reason,' he writes, 'to believe that something material passes from objects to our eyes . . .' (Descartes, 1953, p. 183) 'Light, which is the motion or action of the sun or other bodies we call luminous, pushes a certain very subtle matter contained in all transparent bodies . . .'; but whereas Aristotle had denied that we can see through a vacuum ('Democritus is mistaken in thinking that if the intervening space were empty, even an ant in the sky would be clearly visible; for this is impossible. For vision occurs when the sensitive faculty is acted upon; as it cannot be

the surface of a visible object is seen separately, just as we would separately feel each point's resistance to the stick.

However, the walking-stick analogy is put to very different use in this part of the *Dioptrique*: whereas it served in the earlier discussion to explain Descartes' denial that our ideas of light and colour need resemble their causes, the question whether our idea of position resembles its cause simply does not arise. It is not difficult to see why. Unlike colour-words, 'position' is a word that is strikingly unsuited to ostensive definition. Our primitive archetype for reality corresponding to a word is something that we can point at, but we cannot point at position, any more than we can fail to: and so the question, does a reality correspond to this word? is not one which confronts us.[10] (See Wittgenstein, 1976, pp. 247ff.)

The punctiform analysis of the visible object and the walking-stick analogy together provide Descartes' solution to the problem of the inversion and reversal of the retinal image:

> You must not, therefore, find it strange that objects can be seen in their true position, even though the picture they imprint upon the eye is inverted. This is just like our blind man's being able to feel, at one and the same time, the object B (to his right) by means of his left hand, and the object D (to his left) by means of his right hand. (Descartes, 1953, p. 221; see figure 1)

Descartes' solution is to play down the question, why the world *looks* erect in spite of the inverted retinal image, and to consider instead our capacity to identify, indicate, and situate features of our environment,

acted upon by the actual colour which is seen, there only remains the medium to act upon it, so that some medium must exist; in fact, if the intervening space were void, not merely would accurate vision be impossible, but nothing would be seen at all.' (*De Anima*, 419^{a}15–22)), Descartes denied that there could be a vacuum: 'Concerning the vacuum, in the philosophical sense, that is a space where there is no substance whatsoever, it is clear that there is no such space in the universe, because there is no difference between the extension of space . . . and the extension of body' (Descartes, *Meditations*, p. 620). For a detailed study of Descartes' theory of light, v. Sabra, 1981, chs I and II.

[10] Similarly, 'North' can be ostensively defined, but what about 'bearing'? Of course, I could point to the four cardinal points, and such an explanation might work. But the argument here turns only on what is natural and familiar.

FIGURE 1 Descartes: A man holding two sticks.

treated as points in the visual field. Whether or not it is entirely satisfactory, this solution certainly demonstrates that the problem arose because of the grip of a powerful analogy, and will evaporate as soon as that grip is broken.

I have tried to show that the punctiform analysis of the visible object enabled Alhazen to combine the mathematical theory of vision and intromissionism, and thereby supply the questions to which Kepler's theory of the retinal image was addressed. The cost, as I indicated when I described Alhazen's visual theory, was the problem of the inversion and reversal of the image. Descartes' visual theory was designed to purge Alhazen's punctiform analysis of the visible object, and Kepler's theory of the retinal image, to purge them entirely of their intromissionist dependence on the pictorial analogy. He achieved this by reviving the Stoic analogy, which, like the crux of any good story, is several times overdetermined, and by advancing a causal theory of depiction. His ultimate purpose was to provide one of the pillars of a new scientific enterprise. One of the results was his solution to the problem of the inversion and reversal of the retinal image.

Descartes' solution to this problem is *not* satisfactory precisely because he did not completely break the grip of the pictorial analogy: he failed to distinguish between the retinal image, a natural picture of the visual field, and the irradiation of the retina. An image is visible on the retina because it does not absorb all of the light that strikes it. If the retina were black instead of pink no image would be visible on its surface. This is not to say that the retinal image would no longer be visible because it would be held captive, as it were, by the retina. It is rather to say that there would be no retinal image, since there is no such thing as an invisible image, just as there is no such thing as a non-reflecting mirror. If the retina were black instead of pink there would be no retinal image, although this would not in any way impugn Kepler's description of the optics of the eye.

Kepler's theory of the retinal picture provided a method for calculating which point on the surface of the retina will be struck by radiation from a light source at a given point in the visual field; but whereas the retinal image is visible, although only by means of a fairly complicated apparatus, the irradiation of the retina is not. We cannot see the light radiating from a point in the visual field, refracted by the lens, and gathered to a point on the surface of the retina; neither can we see the consequent electrochemical changes in the nerve-cells of the retina. The retinal image is, trivially, visible; but the irradiation of the retina is not.

The retinal image is caused by the reflection of light which has struck the retina precisely as the theory of the retinal picture predicts. Hence, if we assume that the retina does not absorb all of the light that strikes it, the theory predicts that an inverted and reversed image will be visible on it. By the same token, it predicts that that if the retina is replaced by a thin piece of paper, or something of the sort, an image will be visible on the back of the paper. Thus an experimental confirmation of Kepler's theory was described by Descartes as follows:

> Take an eye from the body of a man who has not been dead long, or failing that, the eye of an ox or another large animal; carefully cut away from its back the three membranes which envelop it, so that a large part of the humour M is uncovered, whilst ensuring that none of it is spilt; then, having covered it again with something that is white and so fine that they daylight passes through it, such as a piece of paper or an egg-shell, RST, fit the eye into a hole made in shutter, Z, so that the front of it, BCD, faces a place where there are various objects, V, X, Y, illuminated by the sun, and the back of it faces into the room, P, where you will be. The only light entering the room should be the light that has travelled through the eye, all of whose parts, from C to S, you know to be transparent. Having done this, you will see on the white body, RST, not perhaps without wonder and pleasure, a picture, depicting vividly and in perspective all the objects outside at VXY . . . (Descartes, 1953, pp. 205–7; see figure 2)

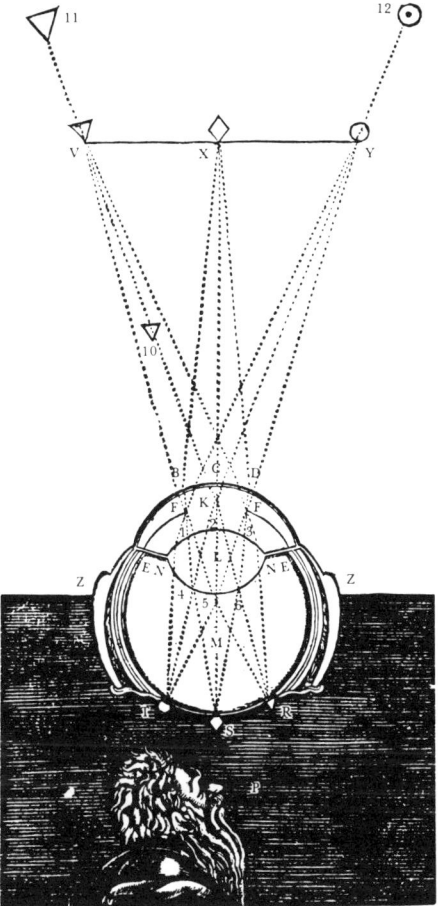

FIGURE 2 Descartes: The geometry of the eye.

The existence of this image, which is inverted but not, of course, reversed, certainly confirms Kepler's theory of the retinal picture.[11] In

[11] An image is reversed if, say, a man who is holding his hat in his left hand appears in the image to be holding his hat in his right hand, and vice versa. If the retinal image of the man is viewed from the front of the eye, he will in fact appear to be holding his hat in his right hand. Thus the image is reversed as well as inverted. But if the image is viewed from behind the eye, as it is in Descartes' experiment, he will appear to be holding his hat in his left hand. (Whether his left hand is on the left side of the image or on its right side is immaterial.)

other words, it confirms that Kepler's description of the optics of the eye was correrct. So does the existence of the inverted and reversed retinal image. However, the retinal image, as opposed to the irradiation of the retina, has no more of a part to play in an explanation of vision than the image produced by following Descartes' instructions.

Thus the theory of the retinal picture did not provide any support for the claims of traditional intromissionism. It was only the failure, by Kepler and his contemporaries, to distinguish between the retinal image and the irradiation of the retina that created the impression that it did. However, since Descartes too failed to draw this distinction, he was compelled to resort to a more desperate measure in order to satisfy his readers that he could consistently embrace the theory of the retinal picture and reject the intromissionist species.

Descartes' solution to this difficulty was a causal theory of depiction. Whereas Kepler had mistaken the retinal stimulus for a picture, Descartes proposed that a picture is simply a visual stimulus. A picture, he maintained, resembles what it depicts only in respect of shape, and even that resemblance is imperfect. Thus whilst engravings may represent to us forests, towns, people, and even battles and storms, they do not do so in virtue of any resemblance between the picture and what it represents. Rather, a picture 'stimulates the mind to conceive the object depicted in it' (Descartes, 1953, p. 203), as a word or a sign stimulates the mind to conceive what it signifies. Indeed, these examples demonstrate that the mind can be stimulated by things that do not resemble what they represent. Retinal images are no different from any other pictures: 'the problem is simply to know how they can enable the soul to be aware of [*sentir*] all the various qualities of the objects to which they correspond, and not in the least to know how they can bear a resemblance to these objects' (p. 204).

Current visual theory is Cartesian in some respects and un-Cartesian in others. The walking-stick analogy is no longer used, but the explanatory pattern that it served to illustrate is adhered to closely where the perception of brightness and colour are concerned,[12] and the

---

[12] Gregory's remarks would command general assent: 'Brightness is an experience . . . Without attempting to explain how physical intensities and wavelengths of radiation give rise to different sensations (and ultimately we do not know the answer) we should realise quite clearly that without life there would be no brightness and no colour . . .

causal theory of depiction commands widespread support. At the same time, the pictorial analogy has not lost its appeal. The next chapter concerns the Cartesian (or causal) theory of depiction. I shall return to the pictorial analogy, and the confusion that it continues to generate, in chapters 3 and 4.

The simplest of the visual sensations is brightness. It is impossible to describe the sensation. A blind man knows nothing of it, and yet to the rest of us reality is made up of brightness and of colour' (1977, pp. 77–8).

2

The Cartesian theory of depiction

Although the Cartesian (or causal) theory of depiction is no longer intended to play the argumentative role for which it was designed, and for which it was in any case unnecessary, it has prospered. But we must distinguish. Whereas certain writers have advanced a causal theory of depiction in general, others have restricted the scope of such a theory either to naturalistic paintings or, still further, to trompe l'oeil paintings. However, the present popularity of all such theories amongst philosophers is largely attributable to the revival, by Grice and Strawson, of the causal theory of perception, a theory which, although its appeal to the scientific community has remained constant since the seventeenth century, had suffered a long period of decline in philosophy.

In the philosophical community, the most influential exponent of the causal theory of depiction is Wollheim. In an essay entitled 'Seeing-as, seeing-in, and Pictorial Representation', his exposition of the theory is explicit and unequivocal. He begins by comparing what he calls 'straightforward perception' with 'a special perceptual capacity' from which the capacity for 'seeing-in', that is the capacity to see what is depicted in a picture, supposedly derives. Whereas straightforward perception is 'the capacity we humans and other animals have of perceiving things present to the senses', the 'special perceptual capacity is something which some animals may share with us but almost certainly most don't, and it allows us to have perceptual experiences of things not present to the senses' (Wollheim, 1980, p. 217).

The comparison that Wollheim makes between straightforward perception and the 'special perceptual capacity' is unintelligible unless taken in conjunction with the causal theory of perception. For 'present to the senses' ordinarily means 'perceptible'. A sound is present to the senses if it is within earshot, and a picture is present to the senses if it is within view. Thus Wollheim would appear to be comparing straightforward perception (of the perceptible) with a special and, on the whole, distinctively human capacity for the perception of the imperceptible, which is absurd. But this construal of his remarks depends upon taking the phrase 'have perceptual experiences of' to mean perceive, which is not how Wollheim intends us to take it. Having said what he means by 'straightforward perception', he continues as follows: 'Any single exercise of this capacity is probably best explained in terms of the occurence of an appropriate perceptual experience and the correct causal link between the experience and the thing or things perceived' (1980, p. 217).

Wollheim's proposal is that pictures afford us 'visions of things not present' (p. 218). A vision in this sense is not a revelation, but a visual experience in the causal theorist's sense, that is a constituent of vision, a mental state which visible objects cause in the sighted. Human beings are blessed with the capacity for unusual visual experiences that have not been caused by what they are experiences of, and a picture will generally cause a sighted human being to have an experience of just this sort. The task of the painter, on this view, is to produce something that will cause in a spectator a particular mental state of this unusual sort.[1] A self-portrait, for example, will cause the painter to have a visual experience of his own face, although this experience will have been caused by the pigments smeared on the canvas. (In this case, the experience could not have been directly caused by what it was an experience of, for one cannot directly see one's own face.)

---

[1] 'Examples of mental states other than thoughts,' writes Wollheim, include perceptual experiences, attacks of dizziness, dreams, and moments of terror, amusement, lust or despair (1984, p. 33). He describes the task of the painter as follows: '[Seeing-in] occurs when someone so modifies or adjusts an external object that, when it is presented to a spectator, he will, other conditions being satisfied, be caused to have, or have by design, visual experiences [of things not present] of a kind intended by the person who modified the object. The modification I have in mind is characteristically brought about by the application of line or colour; the person who brings it about is (in the terminology of this essay) the artist; and we have arrived at pictorial representation' (1980, pp. 218–19).

Both the thought that pictures enable us to have visual experiences of things that are not present to the senses, and Wollheim's 'plausible suggestion' that 'the most primitive instances' of this remarkable capacity 'are to be found in dreams, day-dreams, and hallucinations' (1980, p. 217) have, whatever their merits, the imprimatur of antiquity. In Plato's *Sophist* Socrates says that a painting is a 'man-made dream for waking eyes' (266c); Sextus Empiricus, as I have already observed, records that 'Anaxarchus and Monimus likened existing things to a scene-painting and supposed them to resemble the impressions experienced in sleep and madness'; and Anaxagoras, no less sceptical than Anaxarchus and Monimus, maintained that 'the things apparent are the vision of the things non-evident', a phrase not unlike Wollheim's 'perceptual experiences of things not present to the senses' and his 'visions of things not present'.

I am not suggesting that Wollheim pillaged the works of ancient philosophers. The point of showing that philosophers have always been attracted by the turns of phrase that appeal to Wollheim is to raise the possibility that these phrases give vent to philosophical pressures rather than solving philosophical puzzles. Adapting Wittgenstein, if we are irresistibly inclined, when we surrender ourselves to philosophical thought, to say that pictures, like dreams and hallucinations, afford us the sight of things unseen, 'what we "are tempted to say" in such a case is . . . not philosophy; but it is its raw material' (Wittgenstein, 1958a, §§254 and 299). How are we to determine whether Wollheim's phrase, 'visions of things not present' is, like its ancestors, a metaphor that masks a confusion, or whether it is a solution to a philosophical problem? The answer is simple enough: Wollheim has provided a philosophical account of depiction only if the causal theory of perception is coherent; otherwise, it is just raw material.

Wollheim proposed a causal theory of depiction in general. It is more difficult to identify the intended scope of Gombrich's remark that 'the goal which the artist seeks with such self-critical persistence is . . . a psychological effect' (Gombrich, 1982, p. 228). The psychological effect that Gombrich has in mind is certainly the visual experience which would ordinarily be caused by seeing whatever the artist has depicted. Hence the claim that 'what may make a painting like a distant view through a window is not the fact that the two can be as indistinguishable as is a facsimile from the original: it is in the

similarity between the mental activities both can arouse . . .'
(Gombrich, 1973, p. 240).

Which painters are supposed to be in pursuit of this goal? All
figurative painters; only naturalistic painters; or only those painting
trompe l'oeil? Gombrich's remark is certainly not restricted to painters
of trompe l'oeil, for the painting under consideration is a seascape
hanging on the wall of a museum, which 'we are never tricked into
mistaking . . . for a window opening out on to the real sea' (1973,
p. 194). (No painter in his right mind would try to produce a trompe
l'oeil painting of a seascape.) However, Gombrich is not proposing a
causal theory of depiction in general, for he contrasts painters who
sought to develop 'keys to the lock of our perception' with others,
belonging to a different tradition, who painted in an 'essentially map-
like' style, and produced 'pictographs which tell a story or give an
inventory of stage props': 'many a medieval picture of the sea' would
serve as an example (p. 228).

Is the scope of Gombrich's theory limited to naturalistic painting?
Not quite, for when he suggests that 'the history of art . . . may be
described as the forging of master keys for opening the mysterious
locks of our senses to which only nature herself originally held the
key', Gombrich includes among the inventions in the history of art
'that have something of the character of . . . an open-sesame' the
devices employed by caricaturists (1973, p. 201). Whilst the appreciation
of caricature, to this extent a parasitic genre, requires a familiarity with
naturalistic (or photographic) portraits, caricatures are not themselves
naturalistic pictures.[2] I think we must conclude that Gombrich's theory
is of deliberately inexact scope: his topic is illusion, and illusion, he
contends, 'is always a matter of degree' (p. 196).

Wollheim's theory of depiction and Gombrich's evidently differ in
scope, but neither is intelligible independently of the causal theory of
perception: in this respect they do not differ. In fact, neither of these
writers has actually defended the causal theory of perception; and
neither of the two most distinguished advocates of the causal theory of

[2] The success of a caricature depends on making the distortion of its subject's
features seem entirely natural, because the genre – parodic portraiture – trades on the
confusion of modes of depiction: a caricature is both a naturalistic picture of a
ludicrously ugly person, and a wildly distorted portrait of the person caricatured.

perception in its modern form, Grice and Strawson, has explicitly advocated a causal theory of depiction. However, it does not appear to me possible to defend the causal theory of perception and to repudiate a causal theory of depiction of the least ambitious sort, viz. one restricted to trompe l'oeil, without inconsistency.

The causal theory of perception aims to 'characterize the ordinary notion of perceiving' (Strawson, 1974, p. 143), 'the naive or unsophisticated concept of perception' (ibid., p. 82). The theory proposes that it is part of the meaning of, for example, the perceptual statement 'David saw a woman washing herself' that Bath-sheba, the woman that David saw, was causally responsible for his sensory experience of her. This sensory experience is such as it would be correct to report thus: 'I seem to see a woman washing herself'; or It sensibly seems to me just as if I see a woman washing herself'; or 'It looks to me just as if there were a woman washing herself'.

The most famous story of a trompe l'oeil is surely Pliny's story of the competition between Zeuxis and Parrhasius:

> Zeuxis produced a picture of grapes so successfully represented that birds flew up to the stage buildings; whereupon Parrhasius himself produced such a realistic picture of a curtain that Zeuxis, proud of the verdict of the birds, requested that the curtain should now be drawn and the picture displayed; and when he realised his mistake, with a modesty that did him honour he yielded up the prize, saying that whereas he had deceived birds Parrhasius had deceived him, an artist. (*NH*, XXXV, 65–6)

It is clearly a visual experience to be subject to an illusion; but the curtain, which Zeuxis thought he saw, was neither a visual experience nor a visual (i.e. visible) object. In this respect, there is an analogy between illusion and misperception. I might see a small furry animal and say 'I can see a rabbit': but if the animal turns out to be a small cat, the rabbit was neither what I saw (that was a cat) nor an experience. (What could we mean by saying that a rabbit is an experience?) I mistook a cat for a rabbit, and that is all there is to it.

However, illusions are not simply misperceptions, for illusions typically drive a wedge between perception and judgement. The

Müller–Lyer lines, for example, continue to look as if they were of unequal length, when I am certain that they are not. If it seemed to Zeuxis just as if he saw a curtain only until he had realised his mistake, then Pliny's story is not, after all, a story about a trompe l'oeil. Hence, the causal theorist (of perception) is committed to the view that a trompe l'oeil painting of, say, a broken pane of glass is one that is apt to cause a visual experience such as it would be correct to report thus: 'It seems to me just as if I see a broken pane of glass.' In other words, the causal theorist (of perception) is committed to a causal theory of depiction of the least ambitious sort, viz. one that is restricted to trompe l'oeil. Whether the causal theory of perception implies a causal theory of depiction of wider scope, depends upon the breadth of competence granted to the locutions that are used to report visual experience. Since these locutions are unfamiliar and in Grice's paper provisional, I shall not speculate whether they would correctly report the visual experience of a painting other than a trompe l'oeil.

The causal theory of depiction proposes that pictures cause and hallucinations are visual experiences of things not present to the senses; and the causal theory of perception proposes that to see something is to have a visual experience which was caused by what it is an experience of. These theories are obviously entangled. If the causal theory of perception correctly represents the grammar of perceptual verbs, in other words, if it correctly characterizes the ordinary notion of perceiving, then a causal theory of depiction, if only of the least ambitious sort, must also be right. And if it does not, then a causal theory of depiction, of whatever scope, is unintelligible, because the thought that pictures (all or only some) present us with the sight of things unseen derives whatever sense it has from the causal theory of perception. However, the causal theory of perception gains much of its plausibility from the consideration of aberrant perceptual phenomena, such as illusions and hallucinations. Might it be that the causal theory of perception seems plausible because it is suggested by the turns of phrase that hallucinations and paintings tempt us to employ; and these turns of phrase seem to contain profundities only because they are endorsed by the causal theory of perception?

When Grice explicitly argues for the general causal dependence of our perceptual experiences on the things we take them to be of, he does so by comparing vision and hallucination:

Suppose that it looks to X as if there is a clock on the shelf; what more is required for it to be true to say that X sees a clock on the shelf? There must, one might say, actually be a clock on the shelf which in in X's field of view, before X's eyes. But this does not seem to be enough. For it is logically conceivable that there should be some method by which an expert could make it look to X as if there were a clock on the shelf on occasions when the shelf was empty: there might be some apparatus by which X's cortex could be suitably stimulated, or some technique analogous to post-hypnotic suggestion. If such treatment were applied to X on an occasion when there actually was a clock on the shelf, and if X's impressions were found to continue unchanged when the clock was removed or its position altered, then I think we should be inclined to say that X did not see the clock which was before his eyes, just because we should regard the clock as playing no part in the origination of his impression. Or to leave the realm of fantasy, it might be that it looked to me as if there were a certain sort of pillar in a certain direction at a certain distance, and there might actually be such a pillar in that place; but if, unknown to me, there were a mirror interposed between me and the pillar, which reflected a numerically different though similar pillar, it would certainly be incorrect to say that I saw the first pillar, and correct to say that I saw the second; and it is extremely tempting to explain this linguistic fact by saying that the first pillar was, and the second was not, causally irrelevant to the way things looked to me. (Grice, 1961, p. 142)

The hallucinogenic apparatus in Grice's first story cannot work just anyhow. It cannot, for example, transform the input from a camera into a corresponding pattern of cortical stimulation, since we should then say that X saw with a machine, rather as many people see with spectacles, hear with a hearing-aid or by telephone. Suppose, then, that the machine produces patterns of cortical stimulation at random. On one occasion, however, a patient reports that he can see what is, in fact, before his eyes. (The machine is quite irrelevant. We need only imagine that a man hallucinates regularly at midday. One day, at midday, he acts quite normally. Instead of taking his cup for a cat and stroking it, or taking his coffee for a martini and asking for an olive,

he simply drinks the coffee and behaves, in every way, unexception-
ably.)

Our first thought would be that the machine had broken down.
When somebody who is asked what he can see accurately describes
what is before his eyes, we have no reason, without further evidence, to
doubt that he can see. But Grice has seen to it that we have that further
evidence, for he reports that 'X's impressions were found to continue
unchanged when the clock was removed . . .'. We must therefore
conclude that the machine prevented X from seeing what lay in front of
his eyes, as a blindfold would. Or perhaps the machine was, so to say, a
partial blindfold, which prevented X from seeing anything in a certain
place – on the shelf, in this case.

It is entirely misleading to suggest that X's impression was caused
this way rather than that, as a burning sensation in the throat might be
caused by hot coffee or indigestion, or both. X cannot see the clock on
the shelf because hs is causally constrained from seeing it – by a
machine rather than a blindfold – not because his impression had a
different cause. The hallucination is no part of our reason for denying
that X saw the clock: on the contrary, we are prepared to say that X had
an hallucination only because we have established independently that he
could not see. If the question is, why do we believe that X did not see
the clock?, then it is immaterial that X had an hallucination, and the
hallucinogenic machine, like a conjuror's assistant, is there to distract
our attention from the real business: the amputation of X's visual
capacity, the curtailment of his visual field.

The second story differs only insofar as the protagonist (Grice
himself plays this less dangerous role) is prevented from seeing what is
in front of his eyes by something obstructing his view, rather than by
someone fiddling with his brain. He sees the second pillar in the
mirror; he cannot see the first because it is occluded, by the mirror as it
happens, and it is (logically) impossible to see what is occluded.

That something may be excluded from one's field of view, and that
one may thus be causally constrained from seeing it (or failing to see
it), is news from nowhere. It does not establish that if I do see a clock
or a pillar, my visual experience is caused by the clock or the pillar or
by anything else. If I see a clock or a pillar, then the clock or the pillar
is in my visual field, and I am free from certain causal constraints upon
my visual capacity, such as a blindfold: in short, I have the opportunity

to see it. I cannot (logically) see what I do not have the opportunity to see, and I may be (causally) prevented from having that opportunity in various ways; this is all that Grice has shown.

'Having an hallucination is just like perceiving something.' This is the thought that lies behind Grice's argument, and it is one of those turns of phrase that recalls Wittgenstein's warning:

> Being unable – when we surrender ourselves to philosophical thought – to help saying such-and-such; being irresistibly inclined to say it – does not mean being forced into an *assumption* or having an immediate perception or knowledge of a state of affairs. (Wittgenstein, 1958a, § 299)

If it is something that we are unable to help saying, it is something for which the causal theory has a ready gloss: an hallucination involves a perceptual experience which is identical to the experience that is involved in the corresponding perception. The victim of Grice's experiment has the very same experience when he sees the clock and when he hallucinates: it is the causes of these experiences that differ, and it is in virtue of this difference that one is a perception and the other an hallucination.

'Having an hallucination is just like perceiving something.' The two kinds of experience are so alike that we are prone to mistake one of the former kind for one of the latter; and although we generally believe our eyes and our ears, we might even mistake one of the latter kind for one of the former. For example, the barely audible whine of a television set might seem like tinnitus.

'A is just like B' invites the question, 'How are they alike?' If A and B are varieties of rose, the question may be answered by identifying the perceptual modality of the resemblance (visual, olfactory), and by implication the opportunity conditions for perceiving it (illumination, nothing strong-smelling close by) and the way that it can be discerned (looking, sniffing). But if A and B are sensations, although it makes sense to ask, 'How are they alike?' (same location? same intensity? same character?), the question cannot be answered with a perceptual modality. To say of two sensations that they feel the same is not to indicate the perceptual modality of their resemblance (tactile): it is just to reaffirm that they *are* alike, although they may have been differently caused.

If I hallucinate, and it seems to me just as if I were seeing a rose, and if I later actually see a rose, we may say that these two experiences are just like one another. Of course, they do not *look* alike. Hallucinations are not visibilia; they cannot be illuminated or occluded; and what is not visible cannot be said to look like or unlike anything. The only sense in which it is intelligible to say that the two experiences look alike is the sense in which they may, so long as I am not hallucinating in darkness, look alike *to another*. But there is no reason to believe that I would, invariably, look when hallucinating as I look when I see what lies before my eyes.

Hallucinating and perceiving something are not perceptibly similar, for an hallucination is not perceptible. Are they alike in the way that sensations may be alike? According to the causal theorist, they are: rather as headaches have the same character as toothaches – both are throbbing sensations – an hallucination of a rose and the actual sight of a rose may be said to have, for want of a better word, the same character or content.

This is confused. If I hallucinate, and it seems to me just as if I were seeing a rose, and if I later actually see a rose, the two experiences are alike just insofar as the rose that I seemed to see is like the rose that I later saw. Of course, the rose that I seemed to see and the rose that I later saw do not *look* alike, for I could not look at a rose that I only thought I saw. What, then, does it mean to say that they *are* alike? It does not mean that they have the same phenomenological character: what, other than its perceptible properties, could be meant by the phenomenological character of a rose? Well, they can be similarly described. But in the one case, I am describing a rose, and in the other case, an hallucination, and these are not descriptions *in the same sense*, for my description of an hallucination cannot be mistaken. But surely *this* is incontestible: we use the same form of words. But this only means that the questions 'What did you see?' and 'When you hallucinated, what did you seem to see?' have the same answer.

In short, if one has an hallucination of an M, and later sees an M, one first had an hallucination of what one later saw – regardless of whether, when hallucinating, one believed that one was seeing an M. And this, which appears to be the intelligible residue of the thought that having an hallucination is just like seeing something, is a flat tautology. It is no more illuminating than the observation that if you doubt that p and I affirm that p, then you doubt what I affirm. And of course it does not entail that hallucinating and perceiving involve the occurrence of the same mental item or psychological state.

The argument from hallucination gives us no reason to accept any part of the causal theory of perception. Not only does it fail to establish the putative causal link between our perceptual experiences and what we take them to be of; it does not even establish that there is any intelligible notion of a perceptual experience such that an hallucination of M involves the occurrence of the same experience as perceiving M.

Strawson refined the causal theory of perception, but I shall examine – in some detail – a sentence which is simply intended to convey its overwhelming plausibility.

> We think of perception as a way . . . of informing ourselves about the world of independently existing things: we assume, that is to say, the general reliability of our perceptual experiences; and that assumption is the same as the assumption of a general causal dependence of our perceptual experiences on the independently existing things we take them to be of. (Strawson, 1979, p. 51)

To begin with, I doubt whether the word 'things' is meant to restrict the range of sensibilia to material objects. For as well as objects we can perceive and, in particular, see substances (sugar and syrup), events (the changing of the guard), states (the mess in the kitchen), processes (the burning of London Bridge), nominalized properties (the brilliance of the facade of Rouen cathedral), and so forth. Identifying expressions for all of these can serve to answer the question, 'what did X see?' Hence, 'the world of independently existing things' is presumably another way of saying 'the independently existing world'. Perhaps the entire phrase is redundant. Might we not just as well say: 'We think of perception as a way of informing ourselves'? It is also to be noted that the first assertion trades on the philosophical term of art, 'perception'. Apart from obscuring the differences between sensory modalities, the term does duty for the capacity-term 'sight', as well as 'looking' and 'seeing'. If perception is a way of informing ourselves, 'perception' must be taken to mean looking, not seeing. Of course the grammar of both verbs is very complicated, but take a simple case – discerning the colour of something. Looking is a way of finding out; seeing is not the method or the means, but the achievement. Perhaps this assertion should read as follows: We think of looking (listening, etc.) as a way of informing ourselves.

What is meant, in the second assertion, by the phrase 'the general reliability of our perceptual experiences'? Does Strawson mean that a perceptual experience, like a photograph, is generally a reliable record of its cause? Does he suppose that we examine our perceptual experiences like a detective measuring a footprint?[3] ('Male; five-foot-eleven; 185 pounds; limps on the left foot . . .').

This is absurd. We can no more assume that our perceptual experiences are reliable records of the world of independently existing things than we can compare them with these things to check their veracity. It is perceptual *statements*, not perceptual experiences, that are reliable, the statements of others. An eyewitness is an asset in court because his *testimony* is reliable, if his eyesight is fine and lighting conditions were adequate, if he was neither drowsy nor drunk, etc. A jury will be inclined to assume that his testimony is reliable if it does not conflict with other dependable information, and if they do not question his memory or his motives. I may also say that my *faculties* of sight or hearing are reliable, when I am not tired or feverish; and this will distinguish me from others, shortsighted perhaps, or hard of hearing, or else simply less observant than I. Thus, I might say, 'I found the kitchen by relying on my (generally reliable) sense of smell.' But in this sense of the phrase, we do not all assume the general reliability of our perceptual capacities; those of us who do not believe that our perceptual capacities are generally reliable do not generally assume that they are.

Whilst using our wits, are we continuously assuming that they are reliable? I might prepare a large supper, on the assumption that you will be hungry. Or I might say, 'Assuming it doesn't rain, let's go to the zoo tomorrow'. But in general, we do not assume anything, we act. A sprinter does not assume at every step that the ground will not give

---

[3] The analogy is not a caricature. 'With a single eye,' writes Gregory, 'we generally see the world more or less accurately in three dimensions. For distant objects we use many 'clues' to depth, with a subtlety in the best traditions of the sleuth.' (1974, p. 334)

Somewhat less flamboyantly, Peacocke writes: 'If circumstances are known to be normal, experiences from different angles as of an object as square provide canonical but nonconclusive evidence that it *is* square.' (1983, p. 100)

way beneath him. If I jump out of the way of a bus, it is because I believe something about the bus, not about my perceptual capacities. Of course, a person possesses, say, the capacity to see only if he can generally point to, identify and describe the visible features of his environment, distinguish daylight and darkness, and so forth. However, we do not *assume* that a sighted person can perform these tasks; 'is able to distinguish daylight and darkness' is part of what we *mean* by 'sighted'.

The assertion that we assume the general reliability of our perceptual experiences is surely prompted by the observation that we answer the question, 'How do you know?' by saying 'I saw it!' 'I tasted it!', etc. What is *added* to the assertion that, for example, X murdered Y, if I say, 'I *saw* X murder Y'? An advocate of the causal theory of perception would answer this question as follows: 'I saw X murder Y' is true if and only if X murdered Y, I had a visual experience of X murdering Y, and this visual experience was caused by X murdering Y. I am entitled to assume that this visual experience was appropriately caused, and so I can allude to it in justification either of the claim that X murdered Y, or of the claim that I saw X murder Y.

This answer is misguided. Sentences like 'It seemed to me that I saw X murder Y' are used to withhold or withdraw judgement, and not to justify the assertion that X murdered Y. That is why a jury would be unimpressed by a witness who answered the question, 'How do you know that X murdered Y?', by saying, 'Well, it sensibly seemed to me just as if . . .' One may suspect that this is only because it sounds dubious when what is taken for granted is explicitly stated; but consider whether a statement of the form 'It sensibly seemed to me just as if I saw . . .' could serve to justify the corresponding perceptual statement, 'I saw . . .' Suppose that I say, 'I can see a rabbit', and you say, 'How do you know that you can see a rabbit?' I might answer that I can see its fur, which is of a certain colour, and its ears, which are of a certain length. Of course, this answers the question, 'How do you know that *what* you see is a rabbit?'; but there is no coherent answer to the question, 'How do you know that you can *see* it?' I do not know that I see, rather than smell, a rabbit *any*how; and I do not know that I am not having an hallucination *any*how.

Far from a statement of the form 'It seems to me that . . .' serving to justify the corresponding perceptual statement, perceptual statements commonly serve to justify statements of the form 'It seems to me that . . .' It may seem to me that the baby wants feeding, or that Jeremy is furious; if I say so, then I might justify what I have said by means of a perceptual statement, 'I can hear the baby crying', or 'I can see his eyes blazing'. If the statement 'It sensibly seemed to me just as if I saw X murder Y' cannot be used to justify the corresponding perceptual statement, then the causal theorist cannot consistently maintain that it can be used to justify the statement that X murdered Y, except in a case where a clairvoyant – if such there be – justifies a factual claim by alluding to an experience that was not supposed to have been caused – in the ordinary way, at least – by whatever it was an experience of.

'Z saw X murder Y' entails that X murdered Y. (It also entails that when X murdered Y, X and Y were within Z's field of view, in his visual field. The entailment is important not because we infer that X was within Z's field of view from the fact that Z saw X, but because we infer that Z did not see X from the fact that X was not within Z's field of view.) However, it is a corollary of this entailment that the corresponding perceptual statement cannot corroborate the claim that X murdered Y; and the causal theorist is therefore inclined to seek corroboration elsewhere, in the perceptual experiences of the observer.

If I answer the question, 'How do you know that X murdered Y?', by saying, 'I saw him do it', I am not adducing evidence to support my contention that X murdered Y, although, in seeking my testimony, the prosecution is. *A fortiori*, I am not indirectly adducing as evidence the fact that I have had a particular visual experience. Whatever the corresponding perceptual statement adds to the assertion that X murdered Y, it is not the corroboration of a visual experience, coupled with a causal hypothesis. If counsel puts the question, 'You told the court a moment ago that X and Y were alone in the kitchen at the time of the alleged murder: how then do you know that X murdered Y?' I might answer, 'I was looking through the keyhole; I saw him do it' or else, 'I heard everything from the next room'. These answers do not adduce a perceptual experience to corroborate the accusation of murder; they confirm that I had the *opportunity* to perceive X and Y. If X and Y were visible, then the opportunity conditions obtained for the exercise of my capacity to see; if X and Y were audible, then the opportunity conditions obtained for the exercise of my capacity to hear.

Strawson's remarks provide no reason to believe that the causal theory of perception correctly represents the grammar of perceptual verbs: the smooth transition from one assertion to the next is illusory; the assertions themselves, and the belief that they are equivalent, betray a host of confusions.

The third argument that I shall consider also derives from reflection on aberrant perceptual phenomena. It purports to establish the legitimacy of the causal theorist's notion of visual experiences, and to establish it so patently that the point can be put simply by means of a rhetorical flourish. The argument runs as follows:

> Weiskrantz, Warrington and their colleagues have studied how certain sorts of brain lesions produce what they call 'blind sight'. The patient can give correct answers to questions about visual events and objects that he is presented with, but he claims to have no visual awareness of these objects and events. . . . the patient can in some sense 'see' an object even though he does not have the relevant visual experiences. He simply reports a 'feeling' that something is there, or makes a 'guess' that it is there. Those who doubt the existence of visual experiences . . . might want to ask themselves what it is that we have that such patients lack. (Searle, 1983, p. 47; v. Weiskrantz *et al.*, 1974)

Whilst Grice and Strawson would presumably deny that a blindsighted man is capable of visual perception, precisely because visual experience is a necessary component of vision, Searle suggests that he is capable of visual perception, neither mediated by nor embodied in visual experience: visual experience is not a feature of his mental life, although vision is. This disagreement does not interest me. What does, is that all of these causal theorists would agree that the blindsighted man lacks a constituent of vision, viz., visual experience: it is for the benefit of those 'who doubt the existence of visual experiences' that Searle tells the story of blindsight.

We can devise analogues for blindsight in every perceptual modality. However, not all of these analogues lend themselves to the same argumentative purpose as blindsight. It may therefore be helpful to consider such an analogy; to establish how it differs from the case of blindsight; and to inquire whether this difference provides the support that Searle apparently derives from it. Consider, therefore, an imaginary affliction to be called 'tasteless tasting':

The subject reports that he finds all food entirely tasteless. Eating food is like chewing cardboard. He shows no response to foul-tasting substances. He does not, for example, grimace or spit them out and he expresses no desire to clear his mouth afterwards, say with a glass of water. When asked to identify flavours he performs flawlessly. Formerly a regular contributor to the highly respected journal 'Le Sommelier', he is now completely indifferent to wine, although he retains the capacity to identify, with no less precision than before, any wine (especially a claret) he is given to taste.

In this case, we are not tempted to explain that the patient lacks a *constituent* of gustatory perception. What he lacks is any affective response to flavour. In other words, he is incapable of gustatory pleasure or repugnance.

This disanalogy between blindsight and tasteless tasting reflects a disanalogy between the faculties of sight and taste. We see whether the opportunity conditions for vision obtain, but we feel whether the opportunity conditions for the exercise of the faculty of taste obtain. In the case of vision, but not in the case of taste, we perceive that the opportunity conditions for the exercise of the faculty obtain by exercising that faculty. How this bears upon blindsight is not apparent until we extrapolate from Weiskrantz's experiments to the fictional ideal of blindsight.

The visual capacity of Weiskrantz's subject, D.B., is very limited. He can perform, with varying degrees of success, a variety of crude discriminative tasks such as indicating the approximate direction from which a light is flashed, or distinguishing between horizontal, vertical and diagonal lines. (A detailed analysis of D.B.'s residual capacity may be found in Weiskrantz, 1986.) In short, D.B. has such limited capacities and is so diffident in their exercise that we are not inclined to picture him employing visual skills in the ordinary course of his life. Whilst he can generally point to a light source, he certainly could not make a cup of tea, go to the shops, or keep a watchful eye on the children. But as soon as we consider a fictional ideal of blindsight, a man who could identify and describe objects and their visible properties with the confidence and accuracy of the sighted, whilst denying that he enjoys any visual experience, the question arises, how he behaves in the dark.

Obviously, this is a question which cannot be settled in advance. But the alternatives are clear. Either he will behave as a man suffering from Anton's syndrome behaves in broad daylight,[+] or else he will behave as the normally sighted do in darkness. But unless we assume that he cannot distinguish daylight and darkness we must conclude that the fictional ideal of blindsight, rather like an hysteric, falsely believes that he cannot see. This is clear if we consider a person ideally blindsighted from birth; born, that is, without the capacity for visual experience. Such a person would learn to handle, identify and describe visible objects confidently and accurately *when the opportunity conditions for vision obtain*; but then he could be distinguished from a normally sighted person only on the basis of his behaviour in darkness, and his use of the concepts which pertain to the opportunity conditions for vision – darkness and daylight, and so on.

Searle suggests that 'those who doubt the existence of visual experiences . . . might want to ask themselves what it is that we have that such patients lack'. In one sense, the term 'visual experience' is equivalent to 'vision'. Of a baby born profoundly deaf, one might say: 'He will never have the experience of hearing the birds sing'; but this means no more or less than 'He will never hear the birds sing', or 'He will never be able to enjoy birdsong'. In this sense, to doubt the existence of visual experience would simply be to doubt that anybody sees (or fails to see, or misperceives) anything, which is absurd.

Do the blindsighted lack the capacity for visual experience in this sense; that is, do they lack the capacity to see? As I pointed out, the causal theorists disagree: Searle says no, but Grice and Strawson say yes. However, if the preceeding argument is correct and we *must* assume that the blindsighted behave in darkness as they do in daylight, then the proposition that the blindsighted retain the capacity to see is not false, but senseless. Blindsight is baffling, paradoxical, because the

---

[+] The main characteristic of this condition is the denial of blindness by patients who obviously cannot see. The patients act as though sighted and when attempting to walk they collide with objects, even to the point of injury. Excuses may be offered for their difficulties: 'I lost my spectacles', 'The light is dim', and so forth, or there may be only an indifference to the loss of sight. Unless an ideally blindsighted patient acted in darkness as victims of this condition act in daylight, ideal blindsight is simply the inverse of Anton's syndrome; in other words, the denial of sight by patients who can obviously see.

very question that we feel irresistibly inclined to ask – 'Can the blindsighted see?' – is the one question that we *cannot* ask. The concepts of 'vision', 'perception', and so forth, cannot be used in these exceptional cases, because the preconditions for their application are no longer satisfied.

A correct description of what is before one's eyes, the avowal that one can see it, an appropriate affective response, pointing, indicating whether it is light or dark, simply walking confidently down stairs or across a road – all of these are criteria of visual perception. Generally, these indices of vision go hand in hand, and this background constancy of our interactions with the visible world is part of the framework within which our perceptual statements are made, challenged, altered and confirmed; it is a prerequisite for the application of perceptual concepts. We teach and explain these concepts, and children learn their use against this stable background. In the absence of such constancy we would not employ the perceptual concepts we in fact use; not because they would be incorrect, but simply because the point of using them would be lost. If we did not cry out when hurt, laugh and smile when amused and delighted, then our shared concepts of pain, amusement and delight would get no grip. Wittgenstein reminds us of another example:

> The use of the word 'understand' is based on the fact that in the enormous majority of cases when we have applied certain tests [i.e. asked for and received an explanation of a word], we are able to predict that a man will use the word in question in certain ways. If this were not the case, there would be no point in our using the word 'understand' at all. (Wittgenstein, 1976, p. 23)

If these elementary facts of human nature were to change in imaginable ways, our conceptual structures would collapse.

The difference between tasteless tasting and blindsight is not that in the latter case a constituent of perception is missing. In each case there is a partial satisfaction of the criteria for (gustatory or visual) perception; in each case, the concatenation of skills and regularities of behaviour which forms the basis of our perceptual concepts has been disrupted; but the rupture has occurred at a different point. In the case of tasteless tasting, this rupture does not place a great strain on the relevant perceptual concepts, since affective responses to flavour are among the least uniform of perceptual criteria. In the case of blindsight, the rupture is very much more serious: the concept of vision is useless in such a case. We may choose to greet this circumstance with new terminology; but, as Wittgenstein said, 'by a new notation no facts of geography are changed' (1958b, p. 57). We may, if we wish choose to say that the victim of a certain sort of tumour 'is capable of vision but not of visual experience'. This may be a convenient way of indicating that he is able to perform certain visual tasks but cannot distinguish daylight from darkness and denies that he sees anything. However, we should resist the temptation to pretend that anything is *explained* by this conceptual innovation.

The causal theorist of perception is committed to an account of the phenomenon of blindsight that is confused, and completely misses what is both perplexing and instructive about perceptual aberrations of this sort. But the preceeding discussion of the fictional ideal of blindsight suggests a further argument against the causal theory of perception.

If the causal theory of perception correctly represents the grammar of perceptual verbs, then it is intelligible, however implausible it may be, to suppose that a man might be born without the capacity for visual experiences. Such a man would lack visual experiences whilst satisfying all of the usual criteria for vision. In all the relevant ways, in darkness as well as in daylight, he would behave as the sighted do. He would point out objects whose appearance had caught his attention, and describe them accurately and confidently. He might be a competent and careful driver. The sight of blood might disgust him. And for all this, he would lack the capacity for visual experiences. The imagination balks at this possibility, to be sure; but the question at issue is whether the description of such a case is senseless. For if it is, then so is the causal theory of perception. And to answer this question does not require a fertile imagination.

We can imagine the following note appended to the case report of J.S., a suspected victim of this congenital disorder:

> J.S. is confident and cheerful. I therefore decided to discuss his handicap openly. But when I tried to give him some indication of the great gulf that separates him from the rest of humanity, he refused to accept that he is incapable of having visual experiences.

I explained to him that visual experiences are mental states such as it would be appropriate to report thus: 'I seem to see an F'; or 'It sensibly seems to me just as if I see an F'; or 'It looks to me just as if there were an F'. In reply, he pointed to the trompe l'oeil above my examining couch, and said that it seemed to him just as if he was seeing a broken pane of glass. 'If you are familiar with the causal theory of perception, Doctor,' he added, 'you will understand that the painting is causing me to enjoy a visual experience such as would be caused by a broken pane of glass.' I realized immediately that he did not mean, as we would mean by these words, that the painting was causing him to enjoy a visual experience such as would be caused by a broken pane of glass; for he could not have learned what the term 'visual experience' means. J.S. appears to understand the term 'visual experience', and believes that he understands it; but in fact he cannot understand it. And since it is part of the meaning of a perceptual statement that a visual experience has been caused by a visible object, he cannot understand the ordinary notion of perceiving either. It was then that I realized that our conversation was futile.

The day after examining J.S., an extraordinary and heretical idea occurred to me. J.S. is a celebrated philosopher and, so I believed until I learnt of his sad condition, an advocate of the causal theory of perception. If the theory's other advocates also suffer from this congenital disorder, and we cannot be sure that they do not, what are we to make of the causal theory?

Is the description of a man born without the capacity for visual experiences implausible or unintelligible? (Unless it is intelligible, it is neither plausible nor implausible, since there is no coherent specification of what we might or might not believe.) Nothing could count as evidence for or against the hypothesis that a person has never enjoyed visual experiences; but only somebody who has enjoyed visual experiences can understand the ordinary notion of perceiving. Hence, if the causal theory of perception correctly represents the grammar of perceptual verbs, then a man might use perceptual terms and perceptual statements in a way fitting in with all the usual symptoms and presuppositions of vision, but nevertheless be incapable of understanding the ordinary notion of perceiving. But if the notion of an ability which it is not logically possible to exercise, an ability of which nothing would count as the exercise, is incoherent, then so is the notion of an incapacity which it is not logically possible to betray. As Wittgenstein remarked, 'Here I should like to say: a wheel that can be turned though nothing else moves with it, is not part of the mechanism' (1958a, § 271).

This is not a verificationist argument. In other words, the objection is not that since we shall never know that J.S. lacks, or does not lack, the capacity to have visual experiences, the very notion that he might, or might not, is unintelligible. After all, we shall never know what Shakespeare dreamt the night before he died. The objection is this: the causal theory implies that the concept of a visual or linguistic incapacity which nothing would count as betraying is an intelligible concept; but it is no more intelligible than the concept of an ability – for example, the ability to taste the size of something – of which nothing would count as the exercise. 'The incapacity to have visual experiences' means blindness or else it means nothing at all. The causal theorist would presumably maintain that the case-history of J.S., which uses the phrase 'incapable of having visual experiences' as the causal theory would have us use it, is extremely implausible; but a story that turns upon an unintelligible concept is an unintelligible story. The story of J.S. is an absurd parody of a medical case-history; and the causal theory of perception is an absurd travesty of a theory of perception.

A reader who is tempted by the causal theory of perception, and it *is* tempting, may believe that the arguments against the theory are persuasive, and yet feel dissatisfied for all that. He may feel that something has been missed out; for, when I look at a rose, there is not only the rose but also my seeing it; there is a rose, and something more – *I see*!

In philosophy too, our feelings may lead us astray; and I doubt whether this feeling of dissatisfaction is well founded. The exclamation 'I see!' is supposed to remind us of something that has been left out of account; but can the phrase really perform this task? In class, a child might call out 'I see!' which would be a signal, like raising an arm. In a similar way, I might answer the question 'Where are you?' by calling out 'I'm here!' But the notion that the phrase 'I see!' might simply serve to describe a state of affairs, to identify a psychological experience, makes no more sense than the notion that 'I'm here!' might simply serve to identify my location, without acting as a signal to anyone. It is perfectly meaningless to say, without the context that gives these words a purpose, 'I'm here!'. If I've lost my way, for example, it would scarcely help to remind myself that I'm here. And to say, without a suitable context such as the one described, 'I see!' makes no more sense. It is as if you asked me 'What do you see?' and I answered, with a sweeping gesture, 'I see this!'. To be sure, a man who suddenly recovered his sight might say 'I see!', but to deny the intelligibility of the notion of a perceptual experience, in the sense in which this phrase is used by the causal theorist of perception, is not to repudiate the distinction between the blind and the sighted. It is only to repudiate the intelligibility of a distinction between a sighted man who has visual experiences, in this sense, and the sighted man, J.S., who does not. 'The "private experience"' writes Wittgenstein, 'is a degenerate construction of our grammar . . . And this grammatical monster now fools us: when we wish to do away with it, it seems as though we denied the existence of an experience . . .' (Wittgenstein, 1968, p. 314).

Am I saying that the causal theorist means nothing when he talks about visual experiences? He has got himself into a state of mind in which it is natural to say these things, and 'what we "are tempted to say" in such a case is not philosophy; but it is its raw material.'

The causal theory of perception proposes that to see something is to have a visual experience which was caused by what it is an experience of. If the argument of this chapter is correct, the theory is not coherent; and it follows that the Cartesian (or causal) theory of depiction, which proposes that a picture is an object that causes, in human observers at least, a visual experience of whatever is depicted, is not coherent either. Far from explaining 'what is unique to the seeing appropriate to representations' (Wollheim, 1980, p. 205), the Cartesian theory of depiction is the conjunction of an incoherent theory of perception and an ancient metaphor: a painting, says Socrates, is 'a man-made dream for waking eyes'; the capacity to see what is depicted in a picture, says Wollheim 'allows us to have perceptual experiences of things not present to the senses' (p. 217).[5]

---

[5] Lord Clark used a charming variation of Plato's metaphor to describe his study of *Las Meninas*: 'I would start from as far away as possible,' he wrote, 'when the illusion was complete, and come gradually nearer, until suddenly what had been a hand, and a

A picture is certainly an unusual object of vision. This is evident if one considers the question whether, when looking at a painting, one can see what it depicts. It would of course be misleading to report that one saw the Royal family on a trip to London, on the strength of a visit to the National Portrait Gallery. But this means only that to say that one can see what a painting depicts *means* that one can see the painting, and see that it is a painting of whatever it may be; and it would be a mistake to conclude from this platitude that the question is to be answered in the negative. For, without qualification, that would imply that the features of a depicted scene are *inferred* from the visible features of the painting, the disposition of pigments on the painted surface. And that is certainly false. As I shall argue in a later chapter, this is evident if one considers a pointillist painting that depicts a green lawn by means of a large number of tiny dabs of blue and yellow. Even without any knowledge of optics, I may infer from a close inspection of such a painting that it depicts a green lawn; but standing at a suitable distance, I can *see* that it does. In other words, the answer to the question whether, when looking at a painting, one can see what it depicts depends upon whether the 'what' is construed as a relative or as an interrogative pronoun. If it is construed as a relative pronoun, then the answer is that one cannot; but if it is construed as an interrogative pronoun, then the answer is that one can. The suggestion that pictures afford us 'visions of things not present' betrays a failure to distinguish between the two 'what''s. It is 'what the painting depicts' where the 'what' is an interrogative 'what' that is visible; but it is 'what the painting depicts' where the 'what' is a relative 'what' that is not (necessarily) present, and may well be non-existent.

A picture is an unusual object of vision not because it allows us to see what is not there to be seen, which is absurd, but because when looking at a painting, the natural answer to the question 'What do you see?' is a description of the depicted scene, and not a description of the disposition of pigments. This is not simply because we have learned to assume that this is what the question is after. We can see what is

ribbon and a piece of velvet dissolved into a fricassee of beautiful brushstrokes. I thought I might learn something if I could catch the moment at which this transformation took place, but it proved to be as elusive as the moment between sleeping and waking.'

FIGURE 3 The Müller–Lyer illusion.

depicted; but it is generally more difficult, and it may be very difficult indeed, to see how the pigments are disposed. In other words, it may be very difficult, even impossible, to give the other answer. Many geometrical illusions, which are akin to rudimentary pictures, depend upon this fact. In figure 3, for example, it is easy to see the relation between the lengths of the two thick lines if the question is understood to concern the lengths of parts of the depicted wall; but if the question is understood to concern the marks upon the page that depict these parts of the wall, then most people will be unable to answer it simply by looking – rather than by measurement.

In the next chapter I shall return to the problem of the inversion and reversal of the retinal image.

3

Problem and method

In chapter 1 I sketched a genealogy of the arch-metaphors of visual theory. My purpose was twofold: first, to show that what looks like *a priori* argument in favour of and against ancient physical theories is actually the negotiation of analogies; and second, to describe the manipulation of analogies by means of which Descartes revolutionized visual theory. As I explained, modern visual theory began when Alhazen fragmented the species, the impalpable likeness which was supposed to mediate between a visible object and its visual apprehension, and thereby adapted the pictorial analogy to the mathematical theory of vision. But as the French say, *l'enfant naît en souillures*: Alhazen's ingenious transformation of the pictorial analogy gave rise to a confusion which was regarded for eight centuries as the crux of visual theory.

The problem, in the form that it has taken since Kepler's discovery of the optics of the eye, is this: how is it possible to see the world upright and correctly oriented left and right, despite the fact that the retinal image is inverted and reversed? Recent visual theory has given this problem short shrift: it is generally dismissed in a few lines elaborating Descartes' mockery of traditional intromissionism, and sometimes bolstered by an argument derived from Berkeley. However, the task of the present chapter is to demonstrate that the pictorial analogy continues to entrance visual theorists. The same confusion that underlay the problem of inversion and reversal still exerts its force on visual theorists, like the weight of water against a dam. To be sure, this confusion is no longer betrayed by the problem of inversion and reversal; but this shows only that one hole in the dam has been stopped.

The problem of the inversion and reversal of the retinal image is a paradigm of the sort of problem Wittgenstein had in mind when he wrote the following remark:

> The confusion and barrenness of psychology is not to be explained by calling it a 'young science' . . . For in psychology there are experimental methods and *conceptual confusion* . . .
>
> The existence of the experimental method makes us think we have the means of solving the problems which trouble us; though problem and method pass one another by. (Wittgenstein 1958a, p. 232)

It is not a problem whose solution requires the resources of a laboratory, the imaginative framing of hypotheses, or the accumulation and interpretation of data. Although the question, how upright vision is possible despite the inversion of the retinal image, is one which *appears* to express puzzlement about the causes and explanation of empirical facts, this appearance is misleading. Rather, it is a question which forces itself upon us when the pictorial analogy, regarded simply as a picture, *shaken free of its implication*, holds us captive.[1]

The pictorial analogy is not *mistaken*: analogies are not true or false, although the hypotheses that they may prompt are true or false. Analogies are more or less *useful*. The right hypothesis is the one that is true, but the right analogy is the one that is useful and illuminating. However, it is not my purpose to argue that the pictorial analogy is not, or is no longer, useful to visual theory. I want to show that the pressure exerted by the pictorial analogy, which caused visual theorists to ask the solecistic question, how upright vision is possible despite the inversion of the retinal image, is not dissipated or resisted merely by refusing to take the question seriously. 'The fact that uprightness of vision is achieved despite an inverted retinal image,' writes Irving Rock, 'is a pseudoproblem'[2] (1984, p. 212). Of course, in one sense it

---

[1] In the *Philosophical Investigations* (Wittgenstein, 1958a, § 422), Wittgenstein asks, 'What am I believing in when I believe that men have souls? What am I believing in when I believe that this substance contains two carbon rings? In both cases there is a picture in the foreground, but the sense lies far in the background; that is, the application of the picture is not easy to survey.'

[2] Rock is not the only writer to use the term 'pseudoproblem': v. Boring, 1942, p. 223.

is certainly not a pseudoproblem: centuries of visual theorists did not merely *pretend* to be troubled by it. All that can be meant by 'pseudoproblem' is a problem that is not amenable to experimental solution. It is precisely their impatience with questions of this sort, that is philosophical problems, that has prevented visual theorists in the experimental tradition from extirpating the confusion engendered by the pictorial analogy.

By and large, visual theorists agree that the problem of inversion and reversal arose as the result of what Warnock calls 'a fundamental but oddly tempting mistake'. He continues as follows:

> From speaking of the inverted 'image' on the retina – they sometimes called it a 'picture' – and from pointing out that such an image is always present when anything is seen, they had slipped into thinking that it is this inverted image or picture that we really see. They had the idea of a man living, as it were, behind his own retina, upright inside his own head, peering at the retina as if at a screen on which everything appears upside down. (Warnock, 1953, pp. 29–30)

As far as it goes, this diagnosis is correct. The problem of inversion and reversal betrays a typical homunculus fallacy.[3] But what is the general form of this sort of fallacy, and why is it so tempting here?

The meaning of a word is naturally extended by transferring, for example, a predicate of action from a person to the limb he uses in performing the action. Thus, if I grip the steering wheel one can correctly say that my hands grip it. Similarly, it is natural to employ

---

[3] The term was coined by Anthony Kenny, who quotes Descartes' warning at the beginning of the sixth discourse of the *Dioptrique* (see pp. 8 f) and suggests that Descartes was 'one of the first philosophers to draw attention to the homunculus fallacy' (Kenny, 1984, p. 125). In fact, Descartes' criticism of traditional intromissionism echoes the criticism that Theophrastus makes of Empedocles' theory of hearing: 'It is strange of him to suppose that he has explained how we hear, by merely stating this theory of a sound, as of a gong, within the ear. For suppose that we hear the outer sounds by means of this internal sound; by what do we hear the gong itself, when it rings? For this – the very point of the whole enquiry – is neglected by him.' (Diels, 1879, p. 505)

Plate 1 (left) Duccio, Maesta, *Flagellation*. Siena, Museo dell'Opera del Duomo

Plate 2 (below) Piero della Francesca, *Flagellation*. Urbino, Palazzo Ducale

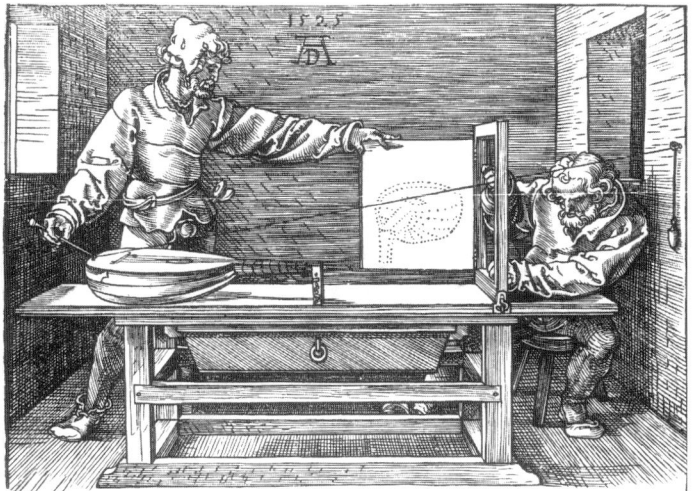

Plate 3 Albrecht
Dürer, from
*Unterweysung der
Messung*, 1525

Plate 4 (above) Nebamun
inspects cattle: New
Kingdom. London,
British Museum

Plate 5 (left) Fragment of
a South Italian vase,
c.380 BC. Würzburg,
Martin von Wagner
Museum

Plate 6 (above) Pollaiuolo, *Frieze of Five Dancers*. Arcetri, Villa Gallina. Detail

Plate 7 (below) Piero della Francesca, *Sacra Conversazione*. Milan, Pinacoteca.
  Detail

Plate 8 (above) Paolo Uccello, *Battle of San Romano*. London, National Gallery.
  Detail

Plate 9 G. B. Piranesi, *Carceri*, Plate VII, second state

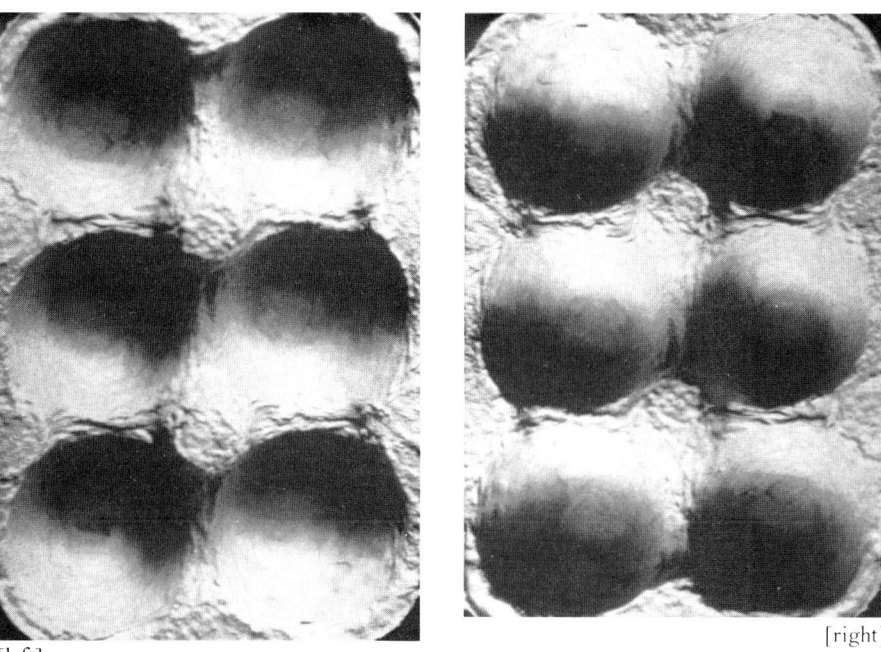

[left] [right]

Plate 10 Egg cartons concave and convex

Plate 11 Hans Holbein the younger, *The Ambassadors*. London, National Gallery

Plate 12 Apostles in the main cupola. Salonika, Haghia Sophia

Plate 13 Apostles in the main apse. Torcello, Cathedral

Plate 14 (above) The prophet Zechariah. Istanbul, Fethiye Camii

Plate 15 (left) Tondo by the Foundry Painter, *c.*470 BC. Munich, Antikensammlungen

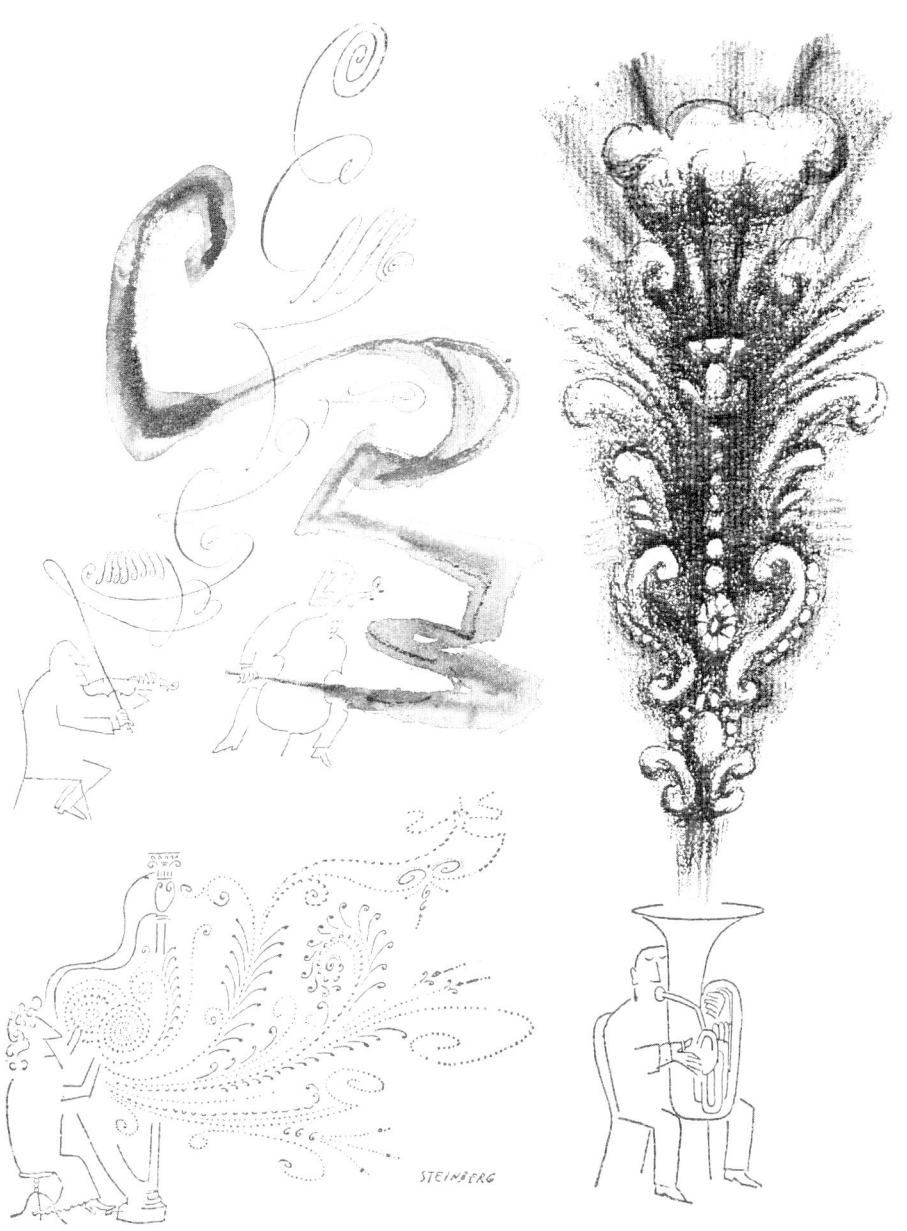

Plate 16 Saul Steinberg, *Musical Instruments*

Plate 17 Koryusai, A Courtesan's Daydream, London, British Museum

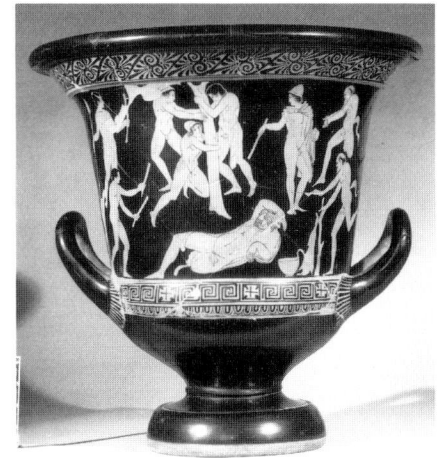

Plate 18 (above) Proto-Attic
amphora by the Polyphemus
Painter, *c*.660 BC. Eleusis
Museum

Plate 19 (right) South Italian calyx
krater with Odysseus and
Polyphemus, *c*.410 BC. London,
British Museum

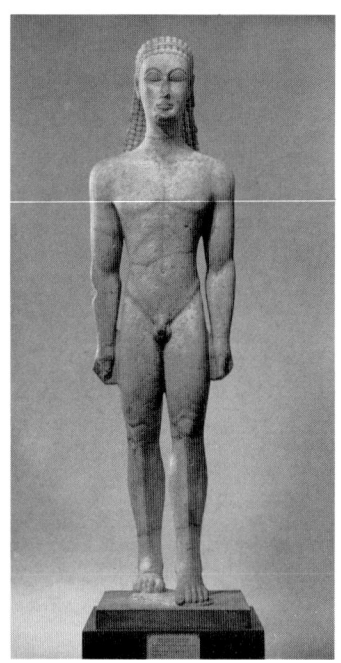

Plate 20 (above) *Kouros*, *c*.600 BC. New York, Metropolitan Museum

Plate 21 (below) The Ram Jug, Proto-Attic. Aegina Museum

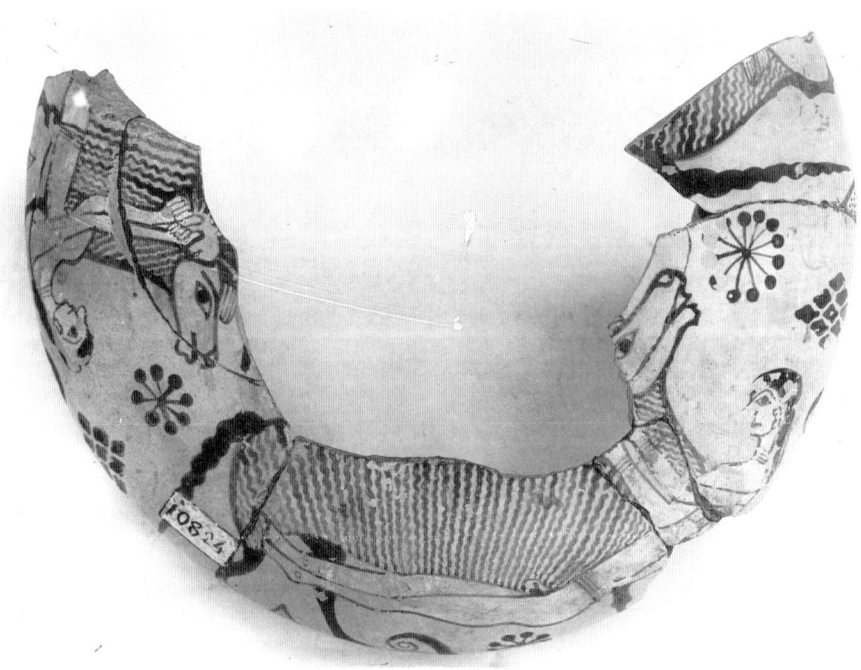

Plate 22 (above) Bird-trapping. Fragment of a wall-painting from the tomb of Nefermaat and Itet at Maidum: Old Kingdom. London, British Museum

Plate 23 (right) Capture of Susa by Assurbanipal, Kuyunjik. London, British Museum

Plate 24 (above) Bayeux Tapestry: *Hic Willelm Dux alloquitur suis militibus ut preparrent se viriliter et sapienter ad prelium contra Anglorum exercitum.* Bayeux, Centre de Guillaume le Conquerant

Plate 25 (below) Bayeux Tapestry: *Hic residet Harold Rex Anglorum. Stigant Archiepiscopus.* Bayeux, Centre de Guillaume le Conquerant

Plate 26 (right) Bayeux
    Tapestry: *Et hic
    Episcopus cibum et potum
    benedicit*. Bayeux, Centre
    de Guillaume le
    Conquerant

Plate 27 (below) Bayeux
    Tapestry: *Hic ceciderunt
    simul Angli et Franci in
    prelio*. Bayeux, Centre
    de Guillaume le
    Conquerant

Plate 28 (right) Wooden relief of
  Hesire: Old Kingdom. Cairo
  Museum

Plate 29 (below) Annunciation
  and Saints. Daphni,
  Catholicon

the name of a perceptual organ to denote the corresponding perceptual capacity or the perceiving subject: 'Mine eyes have seen the glory of the coming of the Lord.' This is a perfectly natural reflection, within the fabric of grammar, of the grammatical truth that interference with the organ characteristically interferes with the exercise of the capacity, and damage to the organ impairs or destroys the capacity. A gourmet is a somebody with a discrimating palate (and a deep pocket), and whilst Samson was literally eyeless in Gaza, a man in 'second childishness and mere oblivion' need not be 'sans eyes' in the sense in which he is 'sans teeth'. Such a change of meaning is not in itself confused.[4] If the speakers of a language adapt a word this way or that, who can gainsay them? However, these natural grammatical configurations are, so to speak, the harmless analogues of the homunculus fallacy.

The homunculus fallacy is committed when predicates that can only intelligibily be attributed to the whole human being are attributed to *parts* of a human being, or to reified human *capacities*. Many predicates may intelligibly be applied both to human beings and to their parts, predicates of size and weight, for instance: it makes sense to infer from the fact that I weigh n stone that my leg weighs less, or from the fact that I am n feet tall that my leg is shorter. However, psychological verbs are unlike these. From the fact that I want something, it not only does not follow that some part of my body wants something (although it may *need* something), but it does not make *sense* to attribute a desire to anything short of the human being (or animal) as a whole. When I am angry or delighted, no part of me is angry or delighted; a contented face is a face that shows a person's contentment, not a face that feels contented.

Verbs of perception, like other psycholocial verbs, apply to the whole human being. It is the person that perceives, and not his brain

---

[4] Wittgenstein castigated Frazer for regarding as confused what he, Wittgenstein, considered to be such movements of meaning: 'When I read Frazer,' writes Wittgenstein, 'I keep wanting to say: All the processes, these changes of meaning, — we have them still here in our word-language. If what is hidden in the last sheaf is called the Corn-wolf, but also the last sheaf itself and also the man who binds it, we recognize in this a movement of language with which we are perfectly familiar.' And he urged that Frazer was wrong to believe that rituals evince mistaken opinions; rather, 'what we have in the ancient rites is the practice of a highly cultivated gesture-language' (1971, pp. 10–11). v. Baker and Hacker, 1980, pp. 469–72, 531–41.

or his perceptual organs. Similarly, it is a fallacy to infer from the fact that I saw or heard something that my brain saw or heard it. Whether a creature perceives something in its environment is determined by its behaviour, by how it responds to what it has perceived, by whether it looks again, sniffs or listens. What occurs in the visual cortex may be a causal condition for seeing, but it makes no sense to suggest that a part of the brain perceives anything.

The scientific study of vision is intended to explain how a physical stimulus which impinges upon the sense organ when the opportunity conditions for the exercise of the perceptual capacity obtain enables the perceiving subject to modify his behaviour in the pursuit of his goals. Of course, this describes the task of contemporary visual theorists: it would be wildly anachronistic to attribute such an aim to Kepler, Alhazen or Democritus. They sought only to identify the form of contact between a visible object and a perceiving subject that permits vision.

The anatomy and physiology of the parts of the body in virtue of which animals possess the capacity to see is the proper object of the scientific study of vision. However, the reduction of a perceptual capacity to its physical basis, the *identification* of the capacity and its physical basis, is not a scientific task or a scientific achievement; it is the heart of the homunculus fallacy. But the pictorial analogy makes it extraordinarily difficult to avoid.

Analogies enable us to represent perspicuously what is already known, and suggest possible ways of pursuing theoretical enquiry. However, as Boltzmann warns, 'the more general the overview one can win, the more surprising the facts one can discover but the more easily too one can fall into error' (Boltzmann, 1974, p. 96). I think that the pictorial analogy has caused such profound and persistent confusion because it compares seeing with a particular *visual* task.

The pictorial analogy compares straightforward visual perception with the indirect visual perception of an object mediated by its mirror image, or by an artificial reproduction of its appearance. Kepler identified the analogue of the mirror image or artificial reproduction as the retinal picture; but what was to be regarded as the analogue of the perceiving subject? Kepler chose the visual faculty, Descartes, who did not free himself entirely from the grip of the pictorial analogy, chose the soul,[5] and more recent theorists, with materialist inclinations, have chosen the visual cortex. Since a perceiving subject is thus an actor in the analogy to the physical process underlying the sense of sight, it is almost inevitable that theorists should have succumbed to the temptation to *identify* the perceiving subject with a reified perceptual capacity or, in the case of recent theorists, with the physical basis of that capacity. The analogy is not in itself misguided, but the confusion it engenders is akin to the confusion of singing, 'Mine eyes have seen the glory of the coming of the Lord', and believing that this can be confirmed with an ophthalmoscope.

As I indicated at the end of the first chapter, Kepler's first error was to identify the analogue of the mirror image or artificial reproduction as the image visible on the retina, rather than the irradiation of the retina which, given that the retina does not absorb all of the light which strikes it, causally explains the existence of the image. This mistake is the first sign that the pictorial analogy is no longer under control, for it indicates that the picture, which plays opposite the perceiving subject in the analogy, has been *identified* with the retinal image and therefore that the distinction between analogy and hypothesis has slipped from view. In other words, it indicates that visual theorists construed the pictorial analogy as a *theory* that postulated the existence of an image in the eye, and regarded Kepler's discovery as a confirmation of the existence of this postulate: the scaffolding has been mistaken for a part of the building. The failure to distinguish between the retinal image and the irradiation of the retina, on the one hand, and the failure to distinguish between the perceiving subject and the (reified) visual faculty (i.e. the homunculus fallacy), on the other, are thus indications of the same underlying confusion, the same failure to distinguish between analogy and hypothesis.

Whilst today's visual theorists are quick to dismiss the problem of inversion and reversal by pointing out that we do not see our retinal images,[6] little interest is shown in the question, why, for eight

---

[5] Thus, in *Les Passions de L'Ame*, Descartes writes: 'There must necessarily be a place where the two images which come through the two eyes . . . (note: '*qui viennent par les deux yeux*'; not, '*qui viennent des deux yeux*') may be united, so that they do not present the soul with two objects instead of one' (Descartes, 1953, p. 711). See also *Traité de L'Homme*, Descartes, 1953, pp. 851–2.

[6] Not all of them: 'The fact,' writes Blakemore 'is, of course, that the subjects of

centuries, visual theorists were troubled by a problem which is so simply dissolved. Scientific students of vision are not expected to understand the history of visual theory and are not trained to do so: and so it should occasion no surprise that they continue to betray the confusions that underlay the problem of inversion and reversal. They have not, for example, learned to distinguish between the irradiation of the retina and the retinal image:

> [Retinal] images are pictures to another observer – someone looking into our eye with a suitable optical instrument – but to ourselves they are but one link in the information chain through the nervous system. We do not see our own retinal images any more than we see the neural activity in the optic nerve or visual regions of the brain.[7] (Gregory, 1970, p. 33)

This is a muddle: my retinal images are not one thing to me and another thing to you, as 25 December might be Christmas to you and Johnny's birthday to me. My retinal images are (natural) pictures which are invisible to me, and visible to another only with a suitable apparatus. They are not analogous to the neural activity in my optic nerve for they are not, as the irradiation of my retina is, causal conditions for seeing.

seeing are not objects themselves, but the flat images of them which hide within the pupil of the eye' (1977, p. 66).

It is worth noting that when the problem of inversion and reversal ceased to trouble visual theorists, this was not because the reasons for the confusions had been understood, even to the extent that they are now understood by visual theorists. The solutions to the problem that were offered in the nineteenth century and in the first half of the present century were derived from Berkeley's *Essay towards a New Theory of Vision* (§§ 88–120) and were largely unintelligible. Helmhotz, for example, did not believe that the inversion and reversal of the retinal image was problematic, and yet he went so far as to claim that we interpret 'the retinal image, of which we are actually conscious' (Helmholtz, 1968, p. 130). He dismisses the problem of inversion and reversal and yet he commits the homunculus fallacy that it betrays as plainly as can be.

[7] D.M. Armstrong makes precisely the same mistake in the following passage: 'When we see, we see *visual objects*, not retinae, the retina remaining completely invisible, and never even thought of "by those unskilful in optics". The inverted retinal image . . . is simply an accompaniment or condition of seeing, it is not what is seen' (Armstrong, 1960, p. 51). The inverted retinal image is indeed an accompaniment of seeing, but it is the irradiation of the retina that is a condition of seeing.

These errors are serious because, as I intend to show, they underly questions which are taken very seriously indeed; in particular, questions pertaining to the perception of size, shape and distance.

'The image of an object doubles in size,' writes Gregory, 'whenever its distance is halved . . . Now what is odd, and it certainly requires explanation, is the fact that although the *image grows* as the distance of the object decreases, *it* [the object] *still looks almost the same size*' (1977, pp. 152–3). If this is odd and requires explanation, Gregory has an explanation to offer: 'We do not see our retinal images,' he writes, 'and we do not see the world according to the size or shapes of the retinal images, for these are effectively modified . . .' (ibid., p. 176): a 'constancy mechanism . . . changes the effective size and shape of retinal images', and this 'subtle scaling mechanism in the brain' (1964, p. 112) enables us to judge correctly the shape and size of visible objects in our environment.[8] 'It keeps the scale of things constant,' writes Gregory, 'in spite of changes of retinal image size with object distance' (1977, p. 152), and changes of retinal image shape with the orientation of the object: he quotes with approval the passage in which Descartes explains that 'our judgements of shape . . . [are] not in accordance with the pictures in the eye; for these pictures

---

[8] This implies that if our perceptual system were simpler we might possess the capacity to learn to respond selectively to objects causing a retinal image of a certain shape or size, without possessing the capacity to learn to respond selectively to objects that have a particular shape or size. Acquiring the latter skill would appear to be a more complex business than acquiring the former skill. This is a view that Quine appears to share: 'Each of a party of observers,' he writes, 'glances at a tile from his own vantage point and calls it square; and each of them has, as his retinal projection of the tile, a scalene quadrilateral which is geometrically dissimilar to everyone else's. The learner of "square" has to take his chances with the rest of society, and he ends up using the word to suit. Association of "square" with just the situations in which retinal projection is square would be simpler to learn, but the more objective usage is, by its very intersubjectivity, what we tend to be exposed to and encouraged in' (Quine, 1960, p. 7).

It is difficult to see what could have prompted this remark except the grip of the pictorial analogy which, as I shall show, caused the problems that the so-called constancy mechanism is designed to solve. After all, if the ease with which we can acquire a skill is the measure of how simple it is to learn, then it is simply false that 'association of "square" with just the situations in which retinal projection is square would be simpler to learn'.

normally contain ovals and diamonds when they cause us to see circles and squares' (Descartes, 1953, p. 224).

The first systematic investigation of constancy was by Robert Thouless in the 1930s. Thouless placed a white cardboard disk at a distance of several metres from his subjects, and asked them to adjust the aperture of a projector until the circular illuminated patch on a screen a few centimetres from their eyes appeared to be the same size as the disk. In another experiment, the subjects were asked to draw the shape of a disk placed at an angle to the line of sight; and in a third, they were asked to choose from amongst a number of cardboard ellipses, varying in eccentricity, the one which appeared to match in shape a disk placed at an angle to the line of sight. These experiments, and others conducted by Gregory, were designed to measure the extent to which the subtle scaling mechanism in the brain modifies the size and shape of retinal images.

Size and shape are visible properties: I can discern the size and shape of a fruit or a rock as easily, and in just the same way, as I can discern its colour, viz., by looking. Of course, it does not always make sense to ask the size or shape of something visible, for not everything that is visible is an object. In other words, not everything that is visible has size and shape. The sky, for example, has no size or shape; rain has no shape, although a raindrop has, and snow has no size, although a snowflake has. Furthermore, not everything that has a determinate size and shape has a visible size and shape. For example, it makes no sense to enquire whether somebody can see the size or shape of a star.

Even in respect of those cases where it makes sense to speak of somebody seeing the shape or size of something, it makes no sense to ask, without further elaboration, whether we are good or bad at these tasks, whether our judgements of size and shape are, on the whole, accurate or not: there is no general answer to be had. Asked how many people could fit around a table with comfort, most of us could answer quite accurately, so long as the table was not too large. But very few of us (with the exception of carpet layers, etc.) could judge the square footage of a room. If, by the capacity to see the size of things, we mean the capacity to make accurate judgements of size on inspection, according to some metric, then we do not possess this capacity, except within a very narrow range.

It is true that we are not often struck by the size of something as we approach it, once we have seen it from a distance. But this does not mean that we have already estimated its size, and our estimate has not proved inaccurate. It means only that we are not often struck by the size of things. It follows that when we are struck, this need not betray a visual incapacity. The colossal scale of the four seated figures at Abu Simbel is visually impressive, whether or not a spectator knows their size. And if the spectator turns away and the looks again, they are still impressive. The question, 'Do you see the size of that skyscraper?' will not generally mean 'Can you accurately estimate its dimensions?', but 'Aren't you impressed by its size?'

Neither is there any general answer to the question, how good we are at perceiving relative size. Presented with a grape and a grapefruit we can immediately see which fruit is the larger, but few of us, if any, could judge with any accuracy how much larger, or how many times larger than the grape the grapefruit is.

How good are we at perceiving shape, and relative shape? Again, there is no general answer. Typical judgements of shape are, for example, 'The plate is octagonal', 'That cloud looks like a camel', 'Johnny has his mother's smile', 'Katy has elegant handwriting'. Whilst a sighted person who has mastered the concept of an octagon will generally be able to identify an octagonal plate, some of us are better than others at discerning family resemblances. Furthermore, perceptual skills like these are not invariably capacities to make *accurate* judgements of shape. It is inaccurate to say that a cloud looks like an Arabian (one-humped) camel if in fact it looks like a Bactrian (two-humped) camel, but if I say of a twelve-sided plate that it is ten-sided, it would be excessively tactful to call my judgement inaccurate, rather than wrong. The notion of accuracy in judgements of shape is not limited to situations of the sort that Thouless artificially created: for example, any drawing that purports to represent the shape of something may be described as accurate or inaccurate, and a competent draughtsman can employ a drawing in order to make a judgement of shape. But the accuracy of a drawing rarely admits of measurement, as opposed to assessment. Similarly, if I describe a person as svelte or skinny, slender or curvaceous, the accuracy of such a judgement can be readily assessed, but it cannot be assessed with precision, as the accuracy of judgements of shape made by Thouless' subjects were assessed with precision, for there is no such thing as a *measure* of the accuracy of such a judgement.

The perceptual skills tested by experiments such as those I have described are very particular skills indeed. Why has so much research been devoted to studying them? Presumably, because psychologists believe that the skills exercised by the subjects of these experiments are, in some sense, *basic* skills, whose possession (along with the possession of linguistic skills, motor skills, and so forth) is an essential prerequisite for the possession of the capacities to identify and describe visible objects and their spatial relations, drive safely and make a cup of tea.

The possession of one capacity may be either logically or empirically necessary for the possession of another capacity. For example, an infant may want feeding, but cannot look forward to tomorrow's food, because mastery of a tensed language is a logical prerequisite for the possession of the capacity to entertain such a thought. It is not unlikely or implausible that an infant will entertain such a thought; it requires no child psychology, no observations and no experiments to determine that an infant cannot entertain such a thought; there is just no such thing as an infant entertaining such a thought. (The mastery of a tensed language is therefore said to be *logically prior* to the capacity to entertain such a thought.) Whereas the ability to run a mile in less than ten minutes may or may not be an empirical prerequisite for the ability to run a marathon, it is a logical prerequisite for the ability to run two miles in ten minutes.

Evidently, the possession of the capacities exercised by the subjects of these experiments is not a logical prerequisite for the possession of the more ordinary capacities. Whether or not it is plausible to suggest that somebody might drive safely and expertly and yet perform no better than chance in these tests, the suggestion is perfectly coherent. However, if the possession of the special capacities is not logically necessary for the possession of the more ordinary capacities, there is as yet no evidence that it is an empirical prerequisite either, for no attempt has been made to correlate relative proficiency at these tasks with more general perceptual skills. Do experiments on size constancy provide data that would be useful in assessing car insurance premiums? In other words, do drivers who perform badly in these tests have more accidents? Do people who perform better in experiments on shape constancy make better graphologists?[9] And if correlations such as these can be established, how, if at all, should they be explained? What, if any, is their correct biological interpretation? As things stand, we just don't know.

What we do know, because it requires no experiment to ascertain, is that the relation between, say, simple and complex motor tasks is not the same as the relation between the special visual tasks performed by the subjects of these experiments, and the ordinary visual tasks performed daily by the sighted. The ability to raise a hand and the ability to make a fist are logically prior to the ability to pour a cup of tea. The simple motor tasks are *components* of the more complex task.[10] However, the task of identifying the shape of the outline of a disk placed at an angle to the line of sight is not a component of the task of pouring tea into a cup. In short, experiments such as those I have described are assessments of very specialized skills. The next question is, what skills are these?

The answer to this question is not, the skills of discerning accurately the sizes and shapes of cardboard disks. (To repeat what the experiments were: in one, Thouless placed a white cardboard disk at a distance of several metres from his subjects, and asked them to adjust the aperture of a projector until the circular illuminated patch on a screen a few centimetres from their eyes appeared to be the same size as the disk; in another, the subjects were asked to draw the shape of a disk placed at an angle to the line of sight; and in a third, they were asked to choose from amongst a number of cardboard ellipses, varying in eccentricy, the one which appeared to match in shape a disk placed at an angle to the line of sight.) In the first experiment, Thouless made quite sure that the subjects would not attempt to match the actual size of the disk by placing the screen so close to them (five centimetres) that an illuminated patch of the size of the disk would virtually fill the visual field. Subjects of the second experiment were unlikely to try to draw

---

[9] One such experiment might measure the correlation between proficiency at the shape constancy test and the minimum number of data points required for the recognition of various pictures.

[10] It is not invariably the case that if the ability to A is logically prior to the ability to B, then A'ing is a component of B'ing: the ability to play chess, for example, is logically prior to the ability to play the Sicilian defence, but playing chess is not a component of playing the Sicilian defence.

the actual shape of the disk (circular, of course): since they were not given the option of identifying it by name, this was evidently not what the psychologists were after. Besides, we are taught to draw a circular object viewed obliquely as an ellipse. In the third experiment, Thouless made sure that subjects would not attempt to match the actual shape of the disk simply by asking them to choose from a number of cardboard *ellipses*.

The answer, which is a straightforward one, is this: the shape experiments assessed the accuracy of a subject's judgement of a disk's outline or silhouette, and the size experiments tested the accuracy of his judgements of what I shall call 'relative occlusion size'. (If I hold out my hands, one closer to my eyes than the other, my hands will not appear to differ in size, but the nearer hand will occlude a larger part of the wall ahead of me than the other.)

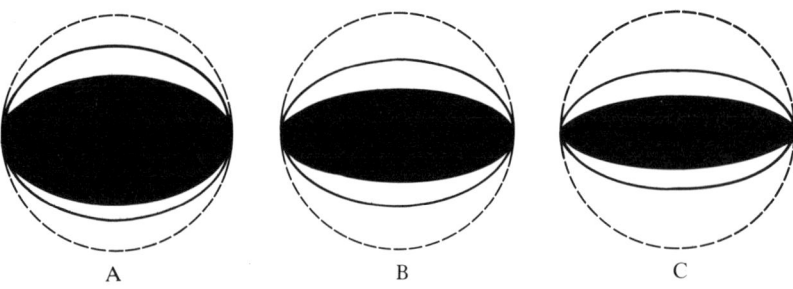

A   B   C

FIGURE 4 Thouless: Phenomenal regression to the real object.

Figure 4 shows, in diagrammatic form, the results of the experiment in which subjects were asked to draw the outline of a disk viewed obliquely. The broken line shows the actual shape of the disk, the black figure shows the actual shape of its outline from the subjects' point of view, and the continuous line shows the mean shape of reproduction. Assuming that Thouless' results are reliable, the shape experiments established that subjects with normal eyesight and without special training tend to make inaccurate judgements of the shape of a disk's outline: they take this shape to be fatter than it is. Similarly, the size experiments established that subjects tend to make inaccurate judgements of relative occlusion size. Such results are not particularly surprising, since we do not get much practice at these tasks.[11] The ability to judge, and the ability to reproduce exactly the shape of an object's outline, or the relative occlusion size of two objects, are not especially useful to most of us. However, they were, until recently, required of a professional painter, and those who lacked a natural aptitude could improve their powers of perceptual discrimination in these, as in other ways. They could, in short, learn to perceive better.

Why is the propensity to make inaccurate judgements of the shape of an outline, and of relative occlusion size, construed as evidence for the existence of a subtle scaling mechanism in the brain which modifies the shape and size of retinal images? The answer to this question is not difficult to find in Thouless' seminal paper, 'Phenomenal Regression to the Real Object':

It is commonly stated in textbooks of psychology that when we observe figures inclined to us, we see them not in the shapes indicated by the laws of perspective but in the shapes which these figures 'really' possess. Thus when we look obliquely at a circular object, we see it not as an ellipse but as a true circle. While it is undoubtedly true that seen in these conditions it is judged to be of its true shape . . . , I do not find that experiment confirms this statement as to what shape is seen. If a subject is shown an inclined circle and is asked to select from a number of figures the one which represents the shape seen by him, he chooses without hesitation an ellipse. This ellipse, however, is widely different from the one which represents the shape of the inclined circle indicated by the laws of perspective, being much nearer to the circular form. The subject sees an inclined figure neither in its 'real' shape nor in the shape which is its perspective projection but as a compromise between these. (Thouless, 1931, p. 339)

[11] Thouless claims that the error is *systematic*, i.e. that occlusion size is generally overestimated, but not underestimated. If this is correct – the experimental evidence is not univocal – one may want to discover why. But this has no bearing on the present argument, which is intended to show that the propensity to make inaccurate judgements of occlusion shape cannot intelligibly be described as a 'phenomenal regression to the real object' and does not constitute evidence for the existence of a scaling mechanism, *whether or not the error is systematic*. An incoherent theory, generated by conceptual confusion, cannot be vindicated by the discovery that the phenomenon requires explanation!

Thouless concludes that in every experiment, 'it was found that what was seen was intermediate between what was given in peripheral stimulation [i.e., the retinal image] and the "real" character of the object' (p. 359). It is clear that the propensity to make inaccurate judgements of the shape of an outline is regarded as evidence for the existence of a scaling mechanism in the brain because these judgements are construed as unimpeachable reports of features of subjective inner experience, and not as inaccurate reports of visible features of the environment. And the argument that persuades visual theorists to construe judgements of the shape of an outline in this way is not difficult to reconstruct.

If a visible object becomes blurred when I take off my spectacles, then the way the object appears to me changes, although the object itself does not undergo any change, and it does not appear to me that it does. In a purely formal sense, one can say that seeming-blurred-to-me is a property of the object, no less than its size or shape, but if I tell you that the appearance of the object has changed, it seems that I am describing my perceptual experience of the object: what has changed is precisely the character of this experience, for my experience is now such as would normally be caused by the object if I were looking at it through a misted window.

Similarly, the apparent shape of an object changes as I move around it, even though the object itself does not undergo any visible change, or appear to me to do so. Hence, my report of the change of the object's apparent shape must surely be a description of my perceptual experience, the causal consequence of the irradiation of my retina. Since the apparent shape of an object differs systematically from its causal antecedent, the retinal image of the object, the causal process which transforms the latter into the former manifestly involves a modification of the shape of the retinal image. Thus Gregory summarizes the results of the shape experiments as follows: 'If you look at [a coin] obliquely,' he writes, 'it will look like an ellipse, but it can be shown that it does not appear as elliptical as the image in the eye. The perception is more like a typical view of the coin from above it.' (1964, p. 112)

If this argument appears cogent, this is partly because it employs different concepts of an object's appearance. In the simplest case, an object's appearance is the sum of its visible properties, and a change in its appearance is an alteration of the sum of its visible properties. But we also employ the concept of how an object appears to a particular spectator. In this case the object's appearance is the sum of its visible properties discernible by that spectator. Thus, an ingenious fake may appear to be a T'ang artefact, but not to me, because I cannot recognize T'ang artefacts. When I take off my spectacles, the appearance of a visible object does not change in the sense in which the appearance of a face may change with make-up. Rather, my capacity to perceive its visible properties is diminished, and I can no longer discern its outline, its contours or the details of its appearance, with any precision. It is natural to call this a change in how it appears to me, although so calling it does not imply that I am inclined to believe that the appearance of the object has changed, that the sum of its visible properties has altered.

However, the concept of appearance employed in the proposition that the appearance of an object changes when I take off my spectacles, is entirely different from the concept of appearance employed in the proposition that the apparent shape of an object changes as we move around it. This is sufficiently clear from the fact that it makes sense to enquire, as Thouless did, whether the apparent shape of an object, its outline, is in general as it appears to a spectator to be (his answer was that it is not), whereas it is senseless to enquire whether or not the blurred appearance of my visible environment when I take off my spectacles is as it appears to me to be. My visible environment appears blurred, but the blurred appearance of my environment appears neither blurred nor distinct.

Judgements of the shape of an object's outline, and judgements of relative occlusion size, however inaccurate, are not reports of features of subjective inner experience.[12] The shape of an object's outline and the relative occlusion size of two objects are visible features of the environment, just as are an object's shape and size.[13] If the temptation

[12] This should be obvious even to those who will accept neither the argument above nor the argument of the last chapter: for we will readily grant that animals might be trained to respond to the shape of an outline, but not that they are able to shift their attention to attain a reflective awareness of the character of their subjective inner experience.

[13] Philosophers interested in vision, no less than their opposite numbers in the laboratory, have mistakenly supposed otherwise. Peacocke is a recent example. He

to think otherwise is derived from the fact that the shape of an object's outline may change although the object itself does not undergo any change, and the relative occlusion size of two objects may change even though neither object undergoes a change of size, this no more shows that the shape of an object's outline, its occlusion size, is a feature of an observer's subjective inner experience, than the fact that the distance between me and the door changes as I walk towards it, without the door moving, shows that the changing distance is a feature of my subjective inner experience.

I have already quoted Gregory's assertion that a coin viewed obliquely does not appear to have the shape of its retinal image: 'The perception,' he avers, 'is more like a typical view of the coin from above it.' It should now be obvious that this remark betrays serious confusion. If the expression 'the perception' is intended to refer to a subjective inner episode, it is nonsensical to compare its shape with the shape of a retinal image or of a coin viewed from above, for subjective inner episodes do not have shapes, or any other visible properties, for they are not visibilia. Moreover, the very mention in this context of the shape of the retinal image is a red herring, even if we read this as the pattern of retinal irradiation. If the word 'transformed' is used somewhat metaphorically, it can be said that the outline of a coin viewed obliquely is generally transformed; but this is just a fancy way of saying that it is generally misperceived; and it is certainly not an *explanation* of this misperception. Another, fancier way of saying the same thing is this: the apparent shape of the outline of a coin viewed obliquely is generally a transformation of the actual shape of its

claims that visual experience has certain features that do not 'represent the environment of the speaker as being in a certain way' (1983, p. 5): 'sensation,' he writes, 'has [a] role to play in . . . visual experience' (p. 8). The claim is backed as follows: 'Suppose you are standing on a road which stretches from you in a straight line to the horizon. There are two trees at the roadside, one a hundred yards from you, the other two hundred. Your experience represents these objects as being of the same physical height and other dimensions; that is, taking your experience at face value you would judge that the trees are roughly the same physical size . . . Yet there is also some sense in which the nearer tree occupies more of your visual field than the more distant tree. This is as much a feature of your experience itself as is its representing the trees as being the same height . . . It is a feature which makes Rock say that the greater size of the retinal image of the nearer tree is not without some reflection in consciousness . . .' (p. 12)

outline. Again, nothing has been explained, and nothing has been added: one form of expression has been replaced by another. But the retinal image of an object has the same shape as the object's outline. Consequently, if the outline of a coin viewed obliquely is misperceived, then the shape that it is wrongly supposed to be will differ from the shape of the coin's retinal image.

We may therefore declare with a flourish that the apparent shape of the outline of a coin viewed obliquely is generally a transformation of the shape of its retinal image. This means: the outline of a coin viewed obliquely, whose shape is identical to the shape of the coin's retinal image, is generally misperceived. It does not mean: there is a subtle scaling mechanism in the brain which modifies the shape of the retinal image.[14] The somewhat tortuous observation that the apparent shape of the outline of a coin viewed obliquely is generally a transformation of the shape of its retinal image *does* add to the mere record of our tendency to misperceive the shape of the outline a certain measure of visual theory: it adds the fact, discovered by Kepler, that the shape of an object's outline is the same as the shape of the natural image of that object, which is visible on the surface of the retina.

I think we must conclude that experiments such as those conducted by Thouless were entirely misconceived. They were designed to test the mainspring of our visual capacities, but did nothing of the sort. Instead they assessed a range of very esoteric skills. To borrow Wittgenstein's words, they exemplify a false exactitude that is the worst enemy of real exactitude. They were though to reveal the neuro-physiological processes which underly the faculty of vision, and transform the retinal image into the virtual replica, or a richly detailed model of the visible environment. Instead they established that, without special training, such as an artist's, we are not much good at visual tasks in which we have little practice, and for which we have little use.

[14] The thought that objects do not appear to have the shapes of their retinal images could only have been prompted by an example such as this, because the two shapes – the shape of the coin and the shape of its retinal image – are readily identifiable and indeed named shapes. A cat, by contrast, is simply cat-shaped; and whilst a cat, unlike an orange, can present any number of aspects, the question, 'Does kitty appear to have the shape of her retinal image, or is this shape effectively modified?' is perfectly unintelligible. Cf. Austin, 1962, pp. 66–7.

The question which Gregory believes can be answered only by postulating a subtle scaling mechanism in the brain is this: how do we see an object as constant in shape and size in spite of the changing shape and size of its retinal image? But this question makes no more sense than the question, how do we see an object as upright, in spite of its inverted retinal image? Both of these questions are indications that the pictorial analogy has got out of hand. The presumption that the brain must adjust the shape and size of the image is no more intelligible than the presumption that it must somehow reinvert it. Objects do not appear to me to have shapes of their representations in my retinal images, but this is not because these images are modified, for the retinal image plays no part in an explanation of vision.

It is true that if I hold my hands in front of me, one twice as far from my eyes as the other, very roughly four times as many retinal cells will be stimulated by light reflected by the nearer hand, as will be stimulated by light reflected by the further hand. But it is also true that a greater number of brain cells fire when the nerve-endings in the tip of one of my fingers are stimulated, than when the nerve-endings in a region of the same size on my forearm are stimulated. This does not mean that there must be a proprioceptive constancy mechanism adjusting either the apparent size of my fingers of the apparent size of my forearm; it explains the greater sensitivity of my fingers. The greater size of the region of the retina irradiated by light from the nearer of two newspapers is not irrelevant to visual theory: it explains the fact that we can read this one, but not the other. Thus visual acuity, the visual analogue of sensitivity, is a function not of actual size, but of visual angle. However, the so-called constancy mechanism is a bad answer to a bad question. In the visual theorists' own terms, problems of constancy are pseudoproblems, and they derive from the grip of the pictorial analogy.

If it is absurd to ask how we are able to see an object as constant in shape and size in spite of the changing shape and size of its retinal image, then a similar absurdity attaches to the question that is supposed to lie at the heart of visual theory concerned with the perception of depth, to wit, how do we see the world in three dimensions although the retinal image is flat? 'The brain', writes Gregory, 'has a most difficult task interpreting retinal information from distant objects. The retinal image has lost a dimension: somehow the brain must construct depth from a projection of three dimensions reduced to two' (1974, pp. 333–4)

What is meant by the proposition that the retinal image has lost a dimension? It does not mean that the retinal image was three-dimensional, but has now been flattened, like a ball of pastry under a rolling-pin. However, it could be said of Matisse that many of his paintings seem to have lost a dimension: with their strong, contrasting colours and conspicuous black outlines, they seem as close as figurative paintings could be to purely ornamental arrangements of flat areas of colour; and his cut-outs seem closer still. In this sense, a picture which reduces three dimensions to two is one that only depicts distance across the picture plane. But the natural image visible on the retina, or on the screen of a camera obscura, is not this sort of picture. So what is meant by the proposition that the retinal image has lost a dimension? Presumably, Gregory means simply that the retinal image, like the image on the screen of a camera obscura and – ignoring impasto – like every figurative painting, is a two-dimensional representation of a three-dimensional scene. 'Although a picture is itself two-dimensional,' he writes, 'it represents objects lying in three dimensions.' (p. 334)

The image visible on the surface of the retina, like a drawing and unlike a sculpture, is flat. But this image, unlike the irradiation of the retina, plays no part in the explanation of vision; and neither the irradiation of the retina nor the consequent changes in the nerve-cells of the retina can intelligibly be described as flat. Thus, the proposition that the brain must construct depth from a projection of three dimensions reduced to two is another indication that the pictorial analogy has got out of hand, for it reflects the notion that seeing is a mattert of discerning the (three-dimensional) subject of a (two-dimensional) picture.[15]

The capacity to discern the distance at which a visible object lies and the capacity to perceive relative distance stand in need of explanation no less than the capacity to discern colour. But the identification of the

[15] It also implies that discerning the subject of a picture is a matter of infusing it with depth. This is not obviously intelligible, for it prompts the question, what are we supposed to infuse with depth, the scene depicted or the painting that depicts it? The scene depicted generally has depth, and so it does not need to be infused with it; but the painting itself is flat and looks flat. The next chapter will consider this matter in detail.

causal conditions for the possession and exercise of these capacities does not consist in the identification of a mechanism which infuses a flat image with depth. Again, the presumption that the brain must infuse the retinal image with depth is no more intelligible than the presumption that it must reinvert it. Ironically, the analogy between problems taxing contemporary visual theorists and the problem of inversion and reversal, far from alerting visual theorists to the confusion which underlies the questions they seek to address, has sometimes led them to the conclusion that the retinal image *is* reinverted: 'A visual perception is not simply a copy of the image on the retina. The image has two dimensions, the perceived object three. The image is upside down, but the object is seen right-side up.' (Held and Richards, 1972, p. 269) (Notice that the inversion of the retinal image has always received more serious consideration than its left-right reversal. Presumably this is because the image will not be left-right reversed if it is viewed from behind!)

It is now well known – Karl Popper recorded the fact – that Hegel purported to prove *a priori* that no planet could be situated between Mars and Jupiter. If this proves that Hegel was a fool (which it does not), then it is no less foolish to try to solve philosophical problems in the laboratory. In this chapter I have endeavoured to show that certain crucial problems in current visual theory are not amenable to experimental solution. Like the problem of inversion and reversal, they betray confusion; they do not express puzzlement about the causes and explanation of empirical facts. Trying to solve these problems by experiment is like trying to dig one's way out of a ditch.

The confusion which has been caused by a grip of the pictorial analogy ramifies into the theory of art. These ramifications are the subject of the next chapter.

4

Art and occlusion

In these two concluding chapters, I shall be concerned with particular moments in the history of Western art, namely the invention of the system of artificial perspective in fifteenth-century Florence (chapter 4) and the inception of naturalism in fifth-century Athens (chapter 5). I intend to show that the conceptual confusions examined in the last three chapters, and others related to them, have precluded a coherent description of these crucial developments in the history of image-making. This will inevitably involve the repetition of certain conclusions and arguments that appear in earlier chapters.

Duccio's *Flagellation of Christ* (plate 1) was painted in the first decade of the fourteenth century; Piero della Francesca painted the same subject one hundred and fifty years later (plage 2). The difference between these paintings that strikes the modern eye most forcibly is in their depiction of the spatial relations between the various parts of the scene: if you hide first the lower and then the upper half of Duccio's painting, Pontius Pilate will leap back and forth. Nothing so indecorous mars the quietude of the later painting. It is well known that this difference is due to the invention, in the 1420s, of the system of artificial perspective; but the character of this achievement has been variously explained. In this chapter, I shall compare the explanation that today enjoys the most widespread support and that which was proposed by the inventors and first exponents of the technique. I shall argue that both of these explanations are confused, and that in each case the confusion derives from the visual theory on which the explanation draws.

There is, however, an antecedent task. The study of vision, as distinct from the ophthalmological study of the eye, was originally stimulated by the apparent disanalogy between sight and touch: the goal of ancient visual theory was to establish what sort of (imperceptible) contact mediates between a visible object and our visual apprehension of it. This, at any rate, was the question that philosophical theories of vision were intended to answer. The mathematical study of vision was, until Alhazen's synthesis, a separate field of study, and the first task of the present chapter, expressed in the most general terms, is to explain what a mathematical study of vision can accomplish. Why is there a geometry of vision, but no geometry of smell or taste?

The mathematical theory of vision, which is also called the theory of perspective, received its first full-fledged exposition in Euclid's *Optica*. Euclid proposed that radiation issues conically from the eye, enabling the percipient to see whatever the visual rays strike. Euclid's theory of vision is thus an extramission theory: radiation is sent from, rather than to, the eye. But the mathematical nature of the theory is more important than its physical implications. The first three postulates state that the rectilinear rays proceeding from the eye diverge indefinitely; that the figure contained by a set of visual rays is a cone of which the vertex is at the eye and the base at the surface of the objects seen; that those things are seen upon which visual rays fall and those things are not seen upon which visual rays do not fall.

The theory of perspective provides a mathematical procedure for determining what is and what is not occluded, i.e. hidden from view, with respect to a given point. it provides a method of calculating what is an what is not *visible*; it is not a means of establishing what is and what is not *seen*. However, the third postulate confuses vision and visibility;[1] and this confusion, far from explaining vision, explains it

---

[1] Writers continue to confuse vision and visibility. 'Our kitchen floor at home,' writes Gombrich, 'happens to have a simple black-and-white checkerboard pattern. As I was taking a glass of water from the tap to the table, *I suddenly noticed* the delightful and interesting distortions of this pattern *visible* through the bottom of the glass. *I had never seen this transformation before*, though I must have made this same movement hundreds of times. . . . I might have taken a hundred or a thousand more glasses from the tap to the kitchen table *without noticing* the appearance of the floor through the bottom of the glass. *Without noticing, not really without seeing.* For of course *I must have seen the pattern before* . . .' Gombrich, pp. 32f; italics added).

The distinction between visibility and vision is obliterated here by decreeing that

away. For the third postulate implies that the question as to whether an object is seen turns only upon its spatial relation to the observer, as if everything that is visible, everything that *can* be seen, *is* seen. Hence what he says and does, indeed what he knows, has no bearing on the question of what he has or has not seen. The observer has rescinded any authority on the question of whether or not he sees something, and the concept of vision has therefore ceased to be the concept of a source of knowledge: looking, in this sense, is no more a way of finding out about the world than is being six hundred yards east-north-east of something.

A theory of vision is a theory that explains how our eyes enables us to learn about the world. The *Optica* is not a theory of this sort. It is a mathematical theory of the angles subtended to the eye by objects in the visual field, a theory of visibility – specifically, of occlusion – and not a theory of vision. The visual field is a cone or pyramid, and thus a given location of the eye corresponds to a particular pyramid of sight, a single array of visual angles subtended by a set of visible objects: the theory of perspective is a geometrical definition of the visual field. In other words, it is a geometrical definition of the concept of occlusion.

There are analogues of occlusion for the other senses: loud music drowns conversation, chilli peppers make it difficult to taste anything else and posies were used to mask the stink of gutters. But of these concepts, only the concept of occlusion is a purely spatial one. Hence, if adequate illumination is taken for granted, and subject to the limitation of distance, it is possible to devise a geometrical procedure for determining whether an object is visible from a given point. That is why there is a geometry of vision, but no geometry of smell or taste.

The system of artificial perspective was invented in Florence in the 1420s. The explanation of its success offered by its advocates places this achievement squarely in the perspectivist tradition initiated by Euclid. The appearance of an object is explained as a function of its spatial relation to an observer. This relation is defined in terms of the angles subtended to the eye. Thus, the identity of the appearance of a scene and its depiction ensured by the system of artificial perspective

whatever is visible is seen. But the distinction may also be obliterated by decreeing that whatever is not seen is not visible. In this case too vision ceases to be a source of knowledge – this time because the observer has, so to speak, appropriated too much authority.

consists in the identity of the angles subtended by the objects in the visual field and the angles subtended by their representations on the picture plane.

The artists of the Renaissance required only a modicum of visual theory in order to use or expound the techniques of artificial perspective. Alberti and Ghiberti, for example, show a certain familiarity with medieval visual theory and appeal to the visual cone or pyramid to justify the geometrical operations by which the visual field is projected onto the picture plane. Alberti describes the picture as a plane intersection of a pyramid of sight, and his vanishing point was at the intersection of the plane with the shortest line from the apex of the pyramid to its base (the so-called centric ray). Little more was clearly understood, but little more was required. 'Among the ancients,' writes Alberti, 'there was no little dispute whether these [visual] rays come from the eye or the plane. This dispute is very difficult and is quite useless for us.' And he adds: 'The function of the eyes in vision need not be considered in this place.' (1966, pp. 46f) The theory of artificial perspective deployed only the mathematics, and not the physics or the physiology of vision, because the verisimilutide of a painting produced in accordance with the rules of artificial perspective was considered to be fully explicable in terms of the geometrical similarity of two visual pyramids, the one between the eye and the picture, and the other between the eye and the scene depicted.

It is still widely believed that the system of artificial perspective provides a method of depicting visible spatial relations which is uniquely successful. But the success of the system is now explained in a manner which its earliest advocates would have found incomprehensible:

> Why should the eye accept a picture as representing objects lying in a space different from its own? It does so because a picture is essentially like a retinal image – both are flat projections of three-dimensional space . . . the brain is so familiar with the problems of adding the third dimension from information given by the flat retinal image that we might expect it to cope with pictures. (Gregory, 1974, p. 335)

The system of artificial perspective is ideally attuned to the visual system's natural skills, it is said, because it makes for pictures just like the pictures we are built to understand: retinal pictures. The system of artificial perspective is simply 'the perspective of retinal images'[2] [ibid., p. 619].

As we have seen, the term 'retinal picture' owes its currency to the tremendous impact of image-making, especially mechanical image-making, upon sixteenth- and seventeenth-century visual theory. Kepler knew that Della Porta regarded the eye as a miniature camera obscura, and in his *Ad Vitellionem Paralipomena* Kepler stated that 'very nearly the same thing occurs [in the eye] as . . . in a closed chamber'. (It was Leonardo who first drew the analogy, but most of his manuscripts were in private hands until 1636, and they were first seriously studied about one hundred and fifty years after that.)

Kepler's interest in visual theory was subservient to his interest in astronomy, and depended upon the analogy between the eye and the camera obscura. In 1600, he explained the puzzling observation, which had been made by Tycho Brahe, that the diameter of the moon appeared to be smaller during a solar eclipse than at other times, although the moon was no further from the earth. Kepler realized that the solution to this puzzle was to be found in optical theory, specifically in the theory of radiation through small apertures; in other words, the error was introduced by the observational instrument. In a letter written to his teacher Maestlin in the following year, Kepler noted that since the eye is an observational instrument possessing an aperture, it too should be prone to such errors. And so the astronomer turned his attention to visual theory.

Although it was directly inspired by the optical study of the camera

---

[2] Rock concurs: 'Indeed,' he writes, 'photographs and drawings are comprehensible to us precisely because they more or less resemble the image of a scene as it appears on our retinas' [Rock, 1984, p. 19) Panofsky held a similar view and anachronistically attributed it to the inventors and first exponents of the system of artificial perspective: 'The painter, however, who has to render three-dimensional objects on a flat surface, that is, to reproduce a visual image appearing in the eye, and not an object existing as a real thing, had to be made familiar with a method of establishing this visual image on a general and scientific basis . . . This is the purpose of the discipline which more than anything else deserves the title of a specific Renaissance achievement: perspective' (Panofsky, 1940, p. 92). A bizarre variant on this idea runs as follows:'[I]n the first stages of visual processing, the brain computes a two-dimensional sketch . . . It looks very much like a rough drawing. (This explains why we can make sense of artists' sketches; they are similar to the symbols computed in our brains.)' (Rosenfeld, 1984, p. 54).

obscura, Kepler's theory of vision was not simply the result of pursuing a fruitful analogy, for it marked the culmination of the perspectivist tradition in medieval visual theory. Skilful ray-geometry, calculated to satisfy the medieval requirement of a one-to-one correspondence between points in the visual field and points in the eye, and focused by the decision to follow Felix Platter in regarding the retina as the principal organ of sight, was orchestrated by the analogy with an image-making machine.

Kepler certainly adapted the pictorial analogy, for the eye was now considered to be an image-*making* machine, rather than an organ for *receiving* images. Nevertheless, his theory of vision was traditional. Like earlier intromissionists, he postulated an indirect connection between the visible object and the observer, a connection that was mediated by an image of the visible object. Following Alhazen, he believed that this image was constructed (or reconstructed) out of the framented, mosaic-like radiation that left the object. Kepler evidently considered that his own achievement in optics was to have located the image in the eye. The inverted and reversed picture painted on the retina just as on the back of a camera obscura was, he believed, the species of the intromissionists.

The retinal image, which is visible only by means of a fairly complex apparatus, is a natural picture which exists because the retina does not absorb all of the light that strikes it. The irradiation of the retina is not visible, but it is, unlike the retinal image, a causally necessary condition for sight.[3] However, as a result of Kepler's optical theory, the confusion generated by the pictorial analogy took a very precise form, namely the failure to distinguish between the retinal image and the irradiation of the retina. I have argued (chapter 3) that this confusion persists even though the problem of inversion and

[3] Aristotle argued that the image reflected by the cornea plays no part in the explanation of vision, but his argument applies equally to the retinal image: 'Democritus . . . is right in his opinion that the eye is of water; not, however, when he goes on to explain seeing as mere mirroring. The mirroring that takes place in an eye is due to the fact that the eye is smooth . . . For the case is merely one of reflection. But it would seem that even in his time there was no scientific knowledge of the general subject of the formation of images and the phenomena of reflection. It is strange too, that it never occurred to him to ask why, if his theory be true, the eye alone sees, while none of the other things in which images are reflected do so.' [*De Sensu*, 2.438ᵃ5–12.]

reversal is no longer taken seriously. It is part of the purpose of the present chapter to show that the explanation of the success of the system of artificial perspective that currently enjoys popularity is little more than an expression of the confusion engendered by the pictorial analogy.

Kepler's theory of vision was purely optical: he did not address the question of how the retinal image enables us to see. But the manner in which he announced his refusal to address this question reveals that he saw non-optical visual theory, no less than the theory of the retinal image, in the light of the pictorial analogy. 'Whether [the retinal image] is made to appear before the soul or tribunal of the visual faculty by a spirit within the hollows of the brain,' he wrote, 'or whether the visual faculty, like a magistrate sent by the soul, goes forth from the administrative chamber of the brain into the optic nerve and the retina to meet this image, as though descending to a lower court – this I leave to be disputed by the physicists.' (Kepler, 1939, pp. 151– 2) Kepler himself had explained how the species is fragmented, how these fragments are conveyed to the eye, and how they are reassembled on the retina; the task that remained, which he left to the physicists, was the task of explaining how the picture is studied and its subject discerned.

The similes that Kepler uses – the magistrates, administrative chambers and so forth – sound quaint and antiquated to us, but we should not be misled: the confusions implicit in this passage persist in the work of contemporary visual theorists. There is no doubt that visual theorists continue to treat the pictorial analogy as if it were an hypothesis, part of which was confirmed by Kepler's optical theory, and part of which remains to be spelt out in detail and subjected to experimental confirmation. Thus a recent book opens with the following sentences: 'What does it mean, to see? The plain man's answer (and Aristotle's too) would be, to know what is where by looking. In other words, vision is the process of discovering from images what is present in the world and where it is.' (Marr, 1982, p. 3) In the same vein, Gregory has declared that 'the ability to read non-optical reality from the optical images in the eyes is the miracle of visual perception' (1970, p. 33). Since the fact that we cannot see our retinal images has not escaped the notice of visual theorists (Pirenne, 1970, p. 9; Gregory, 1970, p. 33), these answers to the question, what is vision? are curiously reminiscent of an old joke: 'What is wireless?' runs the joke, 'Answer: Imagine a dog which is so long that when you pull its tail in Boston it barks in New York. Well, wireless is just like that except without the dog.' 'What is vision?' asks the jesting scientist; 'Answer: You can find out a lot about something by studying a picture of it. (How else would we know about Francis I's extraordinary nose, or Voltaire's extraordinary smile?) If our eyes continuously made pictures of what lay in front of them, we would find out a lot by studying the pictures. Well, vision is just like that, except that we don't see the pictures.'

At this point, we must consider an objection; for it may be argued that although Kepler was certainly misled by the analogy between the eye and an image-making machine, modern visual theorists know very well that neither the brain nor a part of it literally discerns the subject of a retinal image, and will readily explain this metaphor: 'Perceptions are guesses – hypotheses – as to what object has produced the stimulation of the nerves. When we 'see' things, what we see – what is present in the mind – are hypotheses of what object, or kind of object, stimulated the eye.' (Gregory, 1974, p. 616) When a visual theorist suggests that vision is a matter of 'discovering from images what is present in the world and where it is' (Marr, 1982, p. 3), he means nothing more fanciful or implausible than this.

The actors in the drama of vision have certainly changed, for instead of grandiose officials, they are scientsts, eagerly proposing hypotheses and testing them. But the modern version of the story does not dispel confusion; it elaborates it. Certainly, when we see things, what is visible – what is present in the visual field – is causally antecedent to the concurrent irradiation of the retina. But this does not imply that seeing – discerning what is visible – is a matter of ascertaining what has caused the irradiation of the retina. A scientist or a doctor, familiar with modern visual theory, can infer from A's statement that he sees X, that X is currently causing a particular pattern of retinal irradiation in A's eye, and consequent electrochemical changes in the nerve cells of the retina. It is a very different matter to infer that A, or A's brain, or a part of it, infers from these electrochemical changes that X is causing the concurrent irradiation of the retina.[4] This would indeed be

[4] 'Perceptions,' writes Gregory, 'are inferences, based on signalled data from the senses.' (1973, pp. 54f)

something of a miracle: all but a few of us – the doctors and scientists – would be framing hypotheses about the retinal in complete ignorance of visual theory.

The new drama of vision is a variation on a disreputable theme, for it merely elaborates the pictorial analogy for the special case of a *natural* picture. Like a mirror image or the picture produced in a camera obscura, but unlike a painting, which is a product of artifice, the retinal image is a natural picture, and thus discerning what is visible in the picture is identical with establishing its cause. Thus to describe the visual system as interpreting data and framing hypotheses does not explain what is meant by the suggestion that the brain discerns the subject of a retinal picture; it simply carries this mythology one step further. As we shall see, the doctrine that perspective pictures create an illusion of depth because they resemble retinal images is the result of applying this confused conception of sight to the visual perception of spatial relations. And the widespread conviction that the doctrine is sound is therefore further evidence that the pictorial analogy is still a source of confusion in visual theory.

Gregory describes the task of the visual system as follows:

> The brain has a most difficult task interpreting retinal infor-mation . . . The retinal image has lost a dimension: somehow the brain must construct depth from the projection of three dimensions reduced to two. (1974, pp. 333f)

The nature of this task is elucidated by invoking the pictorial analogy: 'One can see why perception of depth is so difficult by thinking about pictures. Although a picture is itself two-dimensional, it represents objects lying in three dimensions' (p. 334). Both retinal images and paintings are two-dimensional representations of a three-dimensional world, and so the task of the visual system is the same in each case. Whether it is confronted by a retinal image or a painting, the visual system must interpret a two-dimensional picture in order to identify its three-dimensional correlate. It is immediately apparent that interpret-ation of the sort that the visual system is imagined to perform is entirely different from the interpretation of a painting, as it is normally conceived. Interpretation is a form of explanation, whether a seismographic record, an enigmatic smile or an Act of Parliament is being interpreted; but whilst the interpretation of a retinal image, like the interpretation of astrophysical data, or the fossil record, is conceived as a causal hypothesis, the interpretation of a painting is not. If one is aware of the relevant iconographic convention, a wheel may enable one to identify a female figure as St Catherine of Alexandria. But the wheel does not play it symbolic role by causal necessity; to interpret this symbol is not to advance a causal hypothesis. The wheel is the symbolic attribute of St Catherine because it is conventionally used as such: it need not be so used, and in an image of Fortuna or Velazquez' *Hilanderas* it is not. And whereas – so we are led to believe – one can identify what the retinal image depicts only as a result of interpreting it, one cannot interpret a motif in a painting without first identifying what it is. Discerning the wheel in the picture is a precondition of offering or contesting any interpretation of its significance, it is not an example of interpretation.

However, Gregory's proposal is that in order to discern the depicted wheel in the first place, the picture must be subject to the same interpretative process as the retinal image of an actual wheel. When one sees an actual wheel, an image of the wheel in perspective is projected onto the retina. Somehow, this pattern of light is interpreted by the brain, which infers from the data furnished by the retina, and transmitted by the optic nerve, that the retina image depicts, i.e. was caused by, a wheel. And when we see a painting of a wheel, the same process enables us to discern the subject of the painting. Hence the greater the similarity between the picture and the retinal image, the greater the similarity between the results of interpretation.

From here it is a short step to the view that perspective paintings create an illusion of depth because they resemble retinal images. However, the claim that the task of the visual system is the same, whether it confronts a painting or a retinal image, implies that whilst we ordinarily perceive features of our environment via the intermediary, as it were, of a retinal image, this is not so when the perceptual object is a picture; in this case we are directly aware of the perceptual object, which mysteriously occupies the place usually assigned to the retinal image.[5] Look at a face, and your brain has the task of interpreting the

<hr/>

[5] 'A painting's value,' writes Gregory, 'depends greatly on the artist and whether it is identified as genuine. It is something of a sacred object, even when its subject is profane. Evidently paintings are regarded as more than surrogate retinal images: they can be valued more highly than sight itself.' (1970, p. 106)

retinal image of a face; but look at a portrait, and your brain has the task of interpreting, not the retinal image of a portrait, but a picture of a face.[6] This is absurd: whatever part the retina plays in vision, it plays it also when we are looking at a picture.

What has gone wrong? The trouble began when ancient theorists of vision proposed that seeing is rather like learning what something looks like by examining a picture of it. Vision is a faculty which enables us to learn about the perceptible environment without contact; and a picture can permit us to discover the appearance of something without seeing it. And so the analogy presents an entrancing *symbol* of the faculty of vision, rather than any sort of theory: it captures the magic of sight rather as certain mythological stories capture the magic of fire or wine. To have misconstrued the analogy as an hypothesis which can be tested, confirmed or confuted was the first and most serious step in the wrong direction. In Kepler's work, the error assumed a more precise form, namely the failure to distinguish between the retinal image and the irradiation of the retina. From then on the confusion was entrenched: the eye makes a picture, and the soul or a part of it, or the brain or a part of it, works out what the picture depicts. By the time visual theorists turned their attention to the

---

[6] The result of this interpretative process, that is the visual experience caused by a picture, is, Gregory suggests, curiously ambivalent, for it comprises two contradictory hypotheses as to what has caused the concurrent retinal image – in the case of a portrait, for example, a painted surface and a person: 'Pictures are objects in their own right – flat patterns of light and shade and colour – while at the same time they are seen as entirely different objects in a different space.' (Gregory, 1970, pp. 50f)

The supposed ambivalence of the visual experience caused by a painting may be a consequence of Gregory's equivocating notion of a picture, which he sometimes conceives as a surrogate retinal image (which would cause a visual experience of what it depicts), and sometimes as a facsimile of a retinal image (which would cause a visual experience of a flat picture). At any rate, when the ambivalence of the visual experience is extended to the painting itself – in a pullulation of absurdity documented in the following quotations – it is obvious that Gregory has simply failed to distinguish between the painted surface and what it depicts. (This confusion has a more interesting variant, which I shall examine in the next chapter.)

(a) '[Pictures] lie perceptually in both two and three dimensions.' (1974, p. 335)

(b) 'No actual object can be both two- and three-dimensional and yet pictures come close to it.' (ibid., p. 365)

(c) 'No object can lie in both two- and three-dimensional space. Yet pictures are both visibly flat and three-dimensional . . . Pictures are impossible.' (1970, p. 32)

problem of artificial perspective, the retinal image had come to be regarded as the very paradigm of a perspicuous image, the easiest sort of picture to understand. It was therefore inevitable that they should have sought to explain the perspicuity of a picture painted in perspective in terms of its resemblance to this paradigm, and have attributed the facility with which we discern the spatial relations in such a painting to the similarity of this task to the correlative task vis-à-vis the retinal image. In other words, pictures painted in perspective are suited to our visual skills because they resemble retinal pictures.

This purported explanation of artificial perspective is a sham. The task of discerning the subject of a painting neither resembles nor fails to resemble the task of interpreting a retinal image: the second task is just a shadow of the first, cast in the light of the visual theorist's analogical imagination. Hence to suggest that we can perform the first task because it resembles the second makes as much sense as explaining that men have two hands because gloves come in pairs. Moreover, if the system of artificial perspective were successful because it makes for pictures that resemble retinal images, then we should expect a similar success to attend the use of a technique proposed by Pieter Camper, in a PhD thesis written in 1746:

> The retina . . . is not equally sensitive in every part. . . . Next to the point of attachment of the optic nerve it is at its most sensitive – and this is the point over against the optic axis . . . (*Corollary* . . . It is clear from this why, in paintings, only one part ought to be lit up and depicted with the greatest distinctness.)[7] (Quoted in Baxandall, 1985, p. 93)

The success of the system of artificial perspective cannot be attributed to the resemblance between the spatial organization of a perspective picture and the retinal picture of an observer who can see whatever the painting depicts. But doesn't this imply that the

---

[7] In the 1970s, Bell Telephone Laboratories, anxious to reduce the bandwidth needed for picturephone transmission, investigated the feasibility of a device which would monitor the gaze of the receiver and send a signal to the transmitting station so that detailed information would be transmitted only for the corresponding region of the screen. The picture would be cheaper to transmit, but it would not be a more accurate picture!

resemblance, which is undeniable, is a coincidence? And isn't this very implausible?

This objection is misconceived. The retinal picture is a natural picture, a reflected image of the observer's visual field. But it is misleading to conceive of a reflective surface, whether a mirror or a retina, as an instrument for producing pictures. If I see a car in my rear view mirror or a ship through the periscope of a submarine, what I perceive is the car or the ship, not a picture of a car or a picture of a ship. To be sure, there is no sharp boundary between the concept of a picture and the concept of an indirect object of perception. Live and recorded television broadcasts do not fall obviously under one concept or the other. But there is no doubt about reflections. We do speak of mirror images, and there is nothing wrong with this turn of phrase, so long as it is understood that to see a mirror image of a car just is indirectly to perceive that car, to perceive it, that is, in the mirror. It is not to perceive something, viz. a particular sort of pictorial representation, on the surface of the mirror, for in order to see the car, it is the car and not the mirror that must be illuminated. And the same goes for the retinal image. Thus, to point out that a picture produced in accordance with the rules of artificial perspective resembles in its spatial organization the retinal image of an observer who can see whatever the painting depicts is simply to reiterate that the system provides a method for depicting the spatial relations between the parts of a scene. The resemblance is not coincidental. After all, it is no coincidence that a mimic who sounds like Churchill will also sound like a recording of Churchill.

If we set aside the analogy between a painting and a retinal image, what is left of Gregory's conception of a painting, and in particular of the depiction of spatial relations? A painting is a 'flat pattern of light and shade and colour' (Gregory, 1979, p. 50), a flat projection of three-dimensional objects: somehow, we restore the lost dimension, and infuse the image with depth.[8] For example, a woodcut by Dürer

---

[8] 'The projection,' writes Gregory, 'is determined simply by the geometry of the situation and this constitutes so-called geometrical perspective.' (1977, p. 163) The reader will recall that Gregory describes pictures as 'flat projections of three-dimensional space' (1973, p. 335); like retinal images, they require the brain to 'construct depth from the projection of three dimensions reduced to two' (pp. 333f).

shows a man drawing a lute (plate 3). We can watch as the lute is compressed onto a plane: when we contemplate a finished drawing, we reverse this process and flesh it out again. The system of artificial perspective is a method of projection from a three-dimensional array onto a (two-dimensional) surface, which ensures that a point on the surface corresponds to every point on the array which is visible from a given point; the spectator deciphers the representation, which yields whatever information could be obtained by observing the array from this point. (In the woodcut, this point is where the string passes through the hook on the wall.) The analogy between a painting and a retinal image was meant to explain why this particular mapping procedure is an essential ingredient in any recipe for naturalistic painting.

This account of the pictorial representation of depth is muddled and self-defeating. The eventual aim was to account for the uniquely successful depiction of spatial relations achieved by the use of the system of artificial perspective; but the result is quite different. Various methods of projection have been used by cartographers. A Mercator projection is generally more useful in navigation than a stereographic map, but it is not more accurate: if the system of artificial perspective is a method of projection from three dimensions to two, then it has no greater claim to verisimilitude than any other system that does the same job with different rules. Gregory cannot coherently maintain that the system of artificial perspective is both a method for producing 'flat projections of three-dimensional space' Gregory, 1974, p. 335, and '[a] solution to the problem of representing three-dimensional objects as realistically as possible' (ibid., p. 619).

Brunelleschi's first demonstration of the system of artificial perspectives was a painting of Santo Giovanni da Firenze. His method, which was later called the *costruzione legittima*, was probably derived from a cartographic technique devised to survey ancient buildings in Rome.[9] At any rate, it was designed as an architects' tool, and was ill-suited to the painter's workshop: it did not provide a method for incorporating human figures into the architectural perspective, and was liable to result in rapid foreshortenings. Above all, it was

[9] Both Brunelleschi's method and Alberti's are described in Krautheimer and Krautheimer-Hess, 1956, ch. XVI.

unwieldy and time-consuming, since it required the preliminary execution of a groundplan and elevations, whether of an actual or an imaginary architectural scene.

The system of artificial perspective explained in Alberti's *De Pictura* was designed to remedy these defects. It is convenient because its use is immediate and independent. Immediate because it does not depend upon a prior specification, by groundplan and elevations, of the scene to be depicted; and independent because it is not a method for representing an actual architectural view in perspective, but rather for ensuring the coherent spatial organization of a view – the plausible choreography of its parts, architectural or not – constructed on the picture plane. In other words, the system of artificial perspective is not a technique for 'compress[ing] three dimensions into two' (Gregory, 1970, p. 33): on the contrary, it is a technique for extending two dimensions to three.

The *costruzione legittima* is rather like a cartographic technique; Alberti's method, in spite of its elaborate geometrical finery, is not. But looking at a perspective painting, however it was produced, is nothing like map-reading.[10] A map can only be read by someone who knows what conventions were used to produce it; but most ten-year-olds who enjoy watching television and are able to decribe Piero della Francesca's painting confidently and accurately, using words such as 'near', 'far', 'above', 'below', 'behind', – most of these children could not understand the system of artificial perspective. Furthermore, the few adults who are familiar with any method of artificial perspective would not cite the rules it comprises to justify a similar description of the painting: citing these rules is not a criterion for seeing what is in a picture, and an inability to cite them is not a criterion for failing to do so. Finally, any attempt to decipher a perspective painting – to treat it like a map – is doomed to failure, since there are indefinitely many three-dimensional correlates of any two-dimensional projection.

Like many twentieth-century writers, Alberti was confused about perspective; like theirs, his confusion is a direct consequence of his

[10] Wittgenstein writes: 'I might get an important message to someone by sending him the picture of a landscape. Does he read it like a blueprint? That is, does he *decipher* it? He looks at it and acts accordingly. He sees rocks, trees, a house, etc. in it.' (Wittgenstein, 1980, § 447)

visual theory. Since he belonged to the perspectivist tradition, Alberti was heir to the error that was inherent in the geometrical theory of vision, viz. the confusion of vision and visibility. The real achievement of the inventors of artificial perspective will become apparent when Alberti's explanation is modified so as to take account of this confusion.

Alberti could not have made head or tail of the modern explanation of perspective. To recapitulate, he believed that the artist strives to reproduce the appearance of what he depicts, and that the system of artificial perspective ensures that the angle subtended by the pictorial representation of an object is the same as the angle subtended by that object. Since he followed the perspectivist tradition in treating the appearance of an object as a function of its spatial relation to an observer, Alberti believed that the verisimilitude of a perspective painting is fully explained by this geometrical similarity. In other words, the geometrical similarity between two pyramids of vision, the one between the eye and the picture and the other between the eye and the scene depicted, ensures that the appearance of the picture and the appearance of the scene are precisely similar.

I have already argued that Euclid's theory of vision is a method of calculating what is and what is not *visible*; it is not a means of establishing what is and what is not *seen*. It is a theory of occlusion, not a theory of vision. We can see what this difference amounts to when Euclid's postulates are amended accordingly.

The third postulate states that the observer sees whatever the visual rays strike and does not see whatever the visual rays do not strike. Since the theory of natural perspective confuses occlusion and vision, this must be amended to state that whatever the visual rays strike is not occluded, and whatever they do not strike, is. Similarly, the fourth postulate must be amended to state that if X subtends a greater angle to the eye than Y, then X will occlude a greater area than Y. This is obviously correct: if I hold two matchboxes before my eyes, one closer than the other, the boxes will not appear to differ in size, but the closer one will occlude a larger part of the wall ahead of me than the other.

The occlusion properties of objects are simply their visible spatial relations. To perceive that one object partially occludes another is just to perceive that the occluding object lies on the straight line between the eye and the part of the further object that is occluded. Similarly, to perceive the greater occlusion size of the nearer matchbox is just to perceive that it is closer to my eye than the other box, and to perceive the elliptical occlusion shape of a disk lying at an angle to the line of sight is just to perceive its orientation. Thus, to depict the occlusion properties of objects is just to depict their spatial relations. The techniques of overlapping (plate 4) and perspective diminution (figure 5; plate 5) create pictorial space because they permit the artist to depict non-planar spatial relations. Overlapping depicts simple occlusion, perspective diminution depicts relative occlusion size and fore-shortening depicts occlusion shape (plate 6), i.e. the shape of an object's outline relative to a certain viewing direction, and hence the object's orientation. Shading (plate 7) is similar to these techniques: whereas foreshortening depicts the orientation of an object relative to the line of sight of the observer, shading depicts its orientation relative to the direction of illumination.

FIGURE 5 Conjectural reconstruction from the Wurzburg skenographic fragment (plate 5).

These occlusion properties and the quasi-occlusion property of relative brightness have been described by Blakemore (1977, p. 40) as 'aspects of the monocular retinal image that can be used by the brain to judge distance'. The techniques employed to depict them are therefore conceived as techniques that will ensure that a painting is like a retinal image. Gregory concurs, and describes occlusion as one of many ' "clues" to depth' that we use 'with a subtlety in the best traditions of the sleuth' (1974, p. 334). This is deeply confused. As I argued in chapter 3, occlusion properties are visible features of the environment, no less than an object's size and shape; and their depiction creates pictorial space not because they are properties of the retinal image from which the brain infers distance, but because the occlusion properties of objects *are* their non-planar spatial relations – to one another, to the observer and to the source of illumination.

Artificial perspective is a systematization of the techniques of overlapping, foreshortening and perspective diminution, based on the theory of natural perspective. Its success cannot be explained in terms of the resemblance between a perspective painting and a retinal image; and its use does not ensure that a painting will reproduce the appearance of what it depicts, as Alberti mistakenly supposed. Quite apart from what has already been said, it is unclear what would count as reproducing the appearance of, say, the Mystical Marriage of St Catherine, if the phrase 'reproducing the appearance' is taken – as Alberti took it – to mean some sort of optical correspondence between the painting and the scene depicted. If, on the other hand, the phrase 'reproduces the appearance' simply means that we *see* what the painting depicts, directly and immediately, then a perspective painting reproduces the appearance of what it depicts in the same way as any other painting.

What the system of artificial perspective achieves is simply the intelligible spatial organization of a depicted scene, the plausible choreography of its parts. The theory of natural perspective enables us to determine what will occlude what, with respect to a given point of observation. The system of artificial perspective is based precisely upon this geometrical theory of occlusion: whatever the visual rays strike is depicted, and whatever the visual rays do not strike is not depicted; if X subtends a greater angle to the eye than Y, then the pictorial representation of X occupies a larger area of the picture plane than Y. By ordering the picture plane in accordance with a system based precisely on the geometrical theory of occlusion, the exponents of artificial perspective gained an exquisite control over the depiction of spatial relations, because *the system of artificial perspective guarantees a consistent pattern of occlusion within the scene depicted*, and thus a consistent pattern of spatial relations between its parts. This is just what Duccio's painting of the flagellation (plate 1) lacks: Pontius Pilate is both in front of and behind the column; his arm occludes part of it, and it occludes part of the platform on which he is standing.

The system of artificial perspective enabled the painter to avoid just this sort of error, however complex the spatial relations depicted, so that a virtuoso could weave a spatial fabric of dazzling intricacy, a sort of three-dimensional jigsaw (plate 8). It also permitted the subtle inconsistencies deliberately hidden – so carefully hidden that one writer has mistakenly suggested that they were an unintended consequence of haste[11] – in Piranesi's *Carceri* (plate 9), which make these architectural monstrosities, literally, impossibly disorientating.

Since occlusion properties are relative to a single point of observation, the cardinal principle of artificial perspective is that a painting is organized in relation to an individual human observer: 'both the beholder and the painted things he sees will appear to be on the same plane' (Alberti, 1966, p. 56). This Protagorean axiom is of some importance in the history of Western Europe's attitude towards images and their manufacture, for it marks a crucial moment in the transition from the mystery of the icon to the secular magic of illusionism. The achievement of illusionism, celebrated in Alberti's injunction to the painter to 'present the forms of things seen on [the picture plane] as if it were of transparent glass' [p. 51], so thoroughly repudiates the material presence of the painting, that the worship of images is no longer possible, leaving room instead for the acclaim of the painter, which the inventors of perspective craved so badly.

[11] 'Some of the ideas poured out so swiftly that . . . he lost himself in the speed of his conceptions.' (Scott, 1975, p. 53)

5

The inception of naturalism

I

Plato's view of the mimetic plastic arts is well known. In Book X of the *Republic* (598) which was written when the process of accretion of naturalistic techniques, which had begun at the end of the Persian wars, was more or less complete, they are condemned wholesale. But there are other passages in the *Republic*, and in other dialogues, which take a more discriminating line. In the *Sophist* (235d–236c), Plato distinguishes between the art of producing a likeness, and the art which produces semblance, but not likeness. A likeness, the Stranger explains, conforms to the proportions of the original in all three dimensions, and gives the proper colour to each part. 'Yes,' says Theaetetus, 'but do not all imitators try to do this?' The dialogue continues as follows:

> *Stranger*: Not those sculptors or painters whose works are of colossal size. If they were to reproduce the true proportions of a well-made figure, as you know, the upper parts would look too small, and the lower too large, because we see the one at a distance, the other close at hand.
>
> *Theaetetus*: That is true.
>
> *Stranger*: So artists, leaving the truth to take care of itself, give their figures, not the real proportions, but those that look right (*καλᾶς*[1]).

[1] The notoriously difficult word '*καλᾶς*' is here usually translated as 'beautiful'. But

Theaetetus: Quite so.

Stranger: The first kind of image, then, being like the original, may fairly be called a likeness (εἰκόνα).

Theaetetus: Yes.

Stranger: And the corresponding subdivision of the art of imitation may be called by the name we used just now – likeness-making (εἰκαστική).

Theaetetus: It may.

Stranger: Now, what are we to call the kind which only appears to be the likeness of a well-made figure because it is not seen from a satisfactory point of view . . . may we not call it a semblance (φάντασμα)?

Theaetetus: By all means.

Stranger: And this is a very extensive class, in painting (ζωραφία) and in imitation of all sorts.

Theaetetus: True.

Stranger: So the best name for the art which creates, not a likeness, but a semblance will be semblance-making (φανταστική).

Theaetetus: Quite so.

This recalls a passage from the *Republic* (420c–d), in which Socrates considers the colours rather than the proportions of a statue: 'Now if we were painting a statue,' he says, 'and were met with the criticism that we were not using the most beautiful colours for the most beautiful parts of the body – for we had not coloured the eyes, the body's most precious feature, purple, but black – we could, I think, reasonably reply as follows: "It is absurd to expect us to represent the beauty of the eye in a way which does not make it look like an eye at all and the same

it seems to me that 'right' provides, in English, the contrast Plato intended between 'the real proportions' and those that will fool a spectator – that is, lead him to suppose that the figure is properly proportioned when a good view would reveal it to be grotesque. This is not to say that 'beautiful' is the wrong translation. These two translations are both correct, since by 'beauty', in respect of proportion, Plato simply meant accordance with a mathematical canon. The sculptor who shared this Pythagorean conception of beauty was Polyclitus. Thus, Lysippus did not merely substitute one canon of proportions for another: he rejected Polyclitus's Pythagoreanism altogether. This is the real significance of the remark recorded by Pliny and reproduced below (p. 94).

is true of the other parts of the body: you should look rather to see whether we have made the whole beautiful by giving each part its proper colour . . ."' The similarity between the two passages is striking; indeed, the phrase 'giving each part its proper colour' ('τὰ προσήκοντα ἐκάστοις ἀποδιδόντες'), is virtually repeated in the passage from the *Sophist* (235e) ('ἀποδιδοὺς τὰ προσήκοντα ἐκάστοις').

It seems that *Sophist* 235–6 deals with the first requirement of likeness-making, and its breach, just as *Republic* 420 deals with the second: what the former says about proportion, the latter says about colour. But the two passages actually serve very different ends. The distinction between two different sorts of imitation enables the stranger to draw an analogy between the deceitful art of *phantastikē technē* and the arguments of the Sophists, who appear to be truthful, but are not; whereas *Republic* 420 is designed to show that the members of a community must enjoy the sort of happiness appropriate to their station: one should not try to make everybody happy by clothing them in purple, and having them lie around the fire on couches. *Sophist* 235–6 and *Republic* 420 do not share the same argumentative purpose: the former is, and the latter is not, concerned with the relation between appearance and reality in the province of the plastic arts. In fact, the passage from the *Sophist* is an elaboration of a remark made by Socrates in *Theaetetus*:

> But now that I've got close to what we're saying, Theaetetus, as if it were a painting (σκιαγράφημα), I do not understand it at all; whereas, as long as I was standing some distance away, it seemed to me that there was something in it. (208e)

This passage from *Theaetetus*, unlike *Sophist* 235–6, refers to the sort of painting which Plato regards as analogous to a deceptive argument with a word which seems to have been coined as a sobriquet for the painter Apollodorus, who was active at the end of the fifth and the beginning of the fourth century BC. The word 'σκιαγραφία' means, literally, 'shadow-painting', and Apollodorus, called 'ὁ σκιαγράφος' (Overbeck, 1868, § 1643), is identified by Plutarch as 'the first of men to discover the dying away (φθορά) and the building up (ἀπόχρωσις) of shadows' (*De Glor. Ath.*, 2). But although it was originally used to refer to the work of a particular painter, or at any rate, the use of a technique invented by a particular painter,[2] 'σκιαγραφία' would appear to have acquired a wider application. The word and its cognates appear often in the dialogues, and another passage from the *Republic* permits us to identify two techniques which characterize the supposedly deceitful art that it denotes:

The same magnitude, I presume, viewed from near and from far does not appear equal.
Why no.
And the same things appear . . . concave and convex, owing to similar errors of vision about colours (see plate 10), and there is obviously every confusion of this sort in our souls. And so painting (σκιαγραφία) in its exploitation of this weakness of our nature falls nothing short of witchcraft . . . (*Rep.*, 602c–d.)

These 'errors of vision' are intended to correspond to the two techniques characteric of *skiagraphia*: respectively, perspective diminution and shading. The technique of shading was probably invented by Apollodorus in the last quarter of the fifth century. There is some disagreement about the invention of perspective diminution, but it seems likely that painted scenery employing perspective diminution (possibly showing the 'towers which crown the city far away' at the beginning of the play *Oedipus at Colonus*) was introduced by Sophocles, and that the technique was perfected by Agatharchus of Samos, when he painted a backcloth for a revival of a play by Aeschylus in the 430s.[3] Vitruvius (*De Architectura*, VII, praef.ii) says that Agatharchus left a commentary on this, which inspired Democritus and Anaxagoras to devise a set of rules for the perspective diminution of buildings painted on scenery.

If *skiagraphia*, painting which employed the techniques of perspective

---

[2] Hesychios says that Apollodorus 'mimicked form through shading and colour' (Overbeck, 1868, § 1646); but Quintilian (*Institutio Oratoria*, XII, x, 4) attributes this innovation to Zeuxis. It may be that Apollodorus was the first painter to use mixed colours, and to merge on coloured region with another, and used rudimentary shading. If so, then Apollodorus 'opened the gates of art which Zeuxis entered' (Pliny, *NH*, XXXV, 61).

[3] This is the solution proposed by Webster, (1970, pp. 13–14), who quotes the line from the beginning of Sophocles' *Oedipus at Colonus* that I have included in parenthesis.

diminution and shading, was the sort of painting that Plato considered to be *phantastikē*, what sort of painting did he regard as *eikastikē*? Although this question cannot be answered with certainty, it is likely that Polygnotus was the traditional painter whose work Plato intended as the contrast with *skiagraphia*. Polygnotus was famous for showing the character (*ethos*) of the men he depicted, precisely the skill that Socrates demanded of the sculptor (v. Xenophon, *Memorabilia*, III. x. 1–5). (Aristotle admired Polygnotus, because of this skill, and because Polygnotus depicted men 'better than ourselves' (*Poetics*, 1448ª5f, and 1450ª27f).) Polygnotus was no *skiagraphos*, and knew neither perspective diminuation nor shading: his technique was basically that of line drawing with even washes for colour. (Quintilan, *Inst. Or.*, XII. x. 3.) This is certainly the technique that Plato approved. Thus, in the *Statesman*, the stranger says: 'Our definition seems like a portrait which is as yet an outline sketch and does not represent the original clearly because it has still to be painted in colours properly balanced with one another.' [277b–c]

In *Sophist* 235–6, the Stranger says that a likeness conforms to the proportions of the original in all three dimensions, and gives the proper colour to each part. Plato considered that these requirements are violated, in the art of painting, by the use, respectively, of perspective diminution and shading. The two requirements are supposed to concern monumental sculpture as well as painting; but the second requirement, which, allegedly, is violated by the use of shading, does not seem pertinent to sculpture at all.

Plato's example of *phantastikē* is a sculpture, exemplifying the violation of the first requirement. The stranger explictly claims that this example of *phantastikē* might just as well be a painting as a sculpture: 'Not those sculptors or painters whose works are of colossal size . . .' However, the claim is not convincing: this was an age of panel painting rather than of murals, and the largest paintings would certainly have been the scene-paintings, which were not seen from below, except by the actors. The most celebrated murals were those in the Lesche (informal meeting place) of the Knidians at Delphi, which depicted scenes of the Trojan War, and those in the Stoa Poikile (painted colonnade) at Athens. Both of these, however, were painted by Polygnotus. (Mikon, Polygnotus's contemporary, also worked on the Stoa.)

Sophist 235–6 is a perplexing passage. The argument purports to apply generally to the mimetic plastic arts, but of the two requirements of likeness-making, the first applies to sculpture but not to painting, and the second applies to painting but not to sculpture. The *skiagraphos* was Plato's favourite analogue of the sophist, and yet he chose a monumental sculpture, illustrating a violation of the first requirement of likeness-making, as the example of *phantastikē*. (Although he does talk about statues being correct or incorrect, beautiful or falling short of beauty (*Laws* 668e–669a), nowhere except in the passage from the *Sophist* does he consider a statue as deceitful in the way that a *skiagraphēma* is often – in the passage quoted from *Theaetetus*, for example – supposed to be deceitful.) I shall argue that these anomalies betray more serious flaws in Plato's conception of naturalistic painting.

I have already pointed out that the largest paintings that Plato and his audience would have seen were scene-paintings. It is therefore likely that 'painters whose works are of colossal size' would have been understood to mean the scene-painters, with whose work the technique of perspective diminution was particularly associated.[4] At any rate, *Republic* 602 confirms what the stranger's claim, that his example of *phantastikē* might just as well be a painting, suggests: Plato considered the use of perspective diminution to be in violation of the first requirement of likeness-making.

Consider a painted panel or vase, which depicts two columns, one further from the spectator than the other (figure 5; plate 5). What relation of size is supposed to present a misleading appearance: the one between the two columns, or the one between the two parts of the painted surface which depict them? The parts of the painting, the patches of pigment which depict the columns, differ in size, but this is perfectly apparent: their relative size is just as it appears to be. The depicted columns, on the other hand, appear to be the same size. They appear to differ in distance from the spectator, but not in height. Is the apparent relation of size between the two depicted columns misleading?

Plato answered this question in the affirmative: *Republic* 602 argues that use of the technique of perspective diminution is deceitful

---

[4] As a result, the term 'σκηνογραφία' ([literally, 'scene painting' or 'stage painting') acquired the technical sense, 'the art of depicting perspective diminution'. For the use of the word 'σκηνογραφία', v. Pollitt, 1974, pp. 230–41.

precisely because it leads us to make judgements of relative size which measurement confutes, just as it confutes the judgements of convexity and concavity that the use of shading leads us to make. But it is senseless to ask whether the equal height of the two depicted columns is apparent, or whether they appear to differ in height, i.e., whether there is a gap between the apparent and actual relative height of the two depicted columns. These questions are unintelligible, because there is *no such thing* as a gap between the apparent and the actual relative height of two depicted columns, since there is no such thing as measuring the height of a depicted column. It is part of the concept of a picture that there is no gap between appearance and reality in a depicted scene. In the determination of the features of a depicted scene, the eye is sovereign. This fact did not escape Michelangelo. Vasari quotes him as saying 'that one must keep one's compasses in one's eyes and not in the hand, for the hands execute, but the eye judges.'

The first requirement of likeness-making is not violated by the use of perspective diminution, for it is literally senseless to require that a painting of a building conform to the proportions of the original (if there is an original) in all three dimensions. Not because a painting is flat: the depicted building is not flat. It is senseless, *if the test of whether this requirement is met is conducted by measurement*, because there is no such thing a measuring the proportions of a depicted building. Or rather, measuring the proportions of a depicted building *just is* measuring the proportions of the original. (Herein lies the distinction between a picture and a map or a blueprint.) But if the test is conducted by inspection, then a painting which employs the technique of perspective diminution may indeed conform to the proportions of the original. An accurate painting will, an inaccurate one will not.

Two columns of equal height – I mean actual columns, not depicted ones – one further from the spectator than the other, may or may not appear equal: this will depend upon the visibility of their distance. But their relative occlusion size is not an obstacle to perceiving their equal height. The technique of perspective diminution is a technique for the depiction of relative occlusion size. Foreshortening depicts occlusion shape. As I argued in chapter 3, these, no less than an object's size and shape, are visible features of the environment; and to perceive that the nearer of my two hands occludes a larger part of the wall ahead of me than the other, or that a shorter pencil at the same distance from the eye will occlude the further of two columns of equal height, is not to misperceive the size of my hands or the height of the columns.

The technique of perspective diminution is not analogous to the distortion of the proportions of a monumental sculpture, because the spectator need not misperceive any feature of the medium in order to perceive correctly the spatial relation depicted by means of the technique. The pictorial analogue of Plato's example is a painting designed to be seen from an eccentric point of view, for example, the celebrated anamorphosis at the bottom of Hans Holbein's painting *The Ambassadors* (plate 11). This was intended as a display of virtuosity; but anamorphosis, unlike the technique of perspective diminution, played a serious part in Byzantine church decoration. For example, the legs of the Apostles in the main cupola of Haghia Sophia, Thessalonica (plate 12) are elongated because, whereas the upper parts of the figures lie almost perpendicular to the spectator's line of sight, the lower parts of the figures are more nearly vertical. Figures on the outer edges of the semicylindrical niches of the main apses are broader for a similar reason (plate 13; v. Demus, 1948, pp. 30–4).

Similarly, the technique of shading does not require the spectator to misperceive the colour of pigment, in order to perceive correctly the concavity or convexity that may be depicted by means of it; although it is perfectly possible to mistake an unevenly coloured surface for an evenly coloured plastic form, whether or not the coloured surface is a picture. The pictorial technique that seems to violate Plato's second requirement of likeness-making, as the distortion of the proportions of a monumental sculpture seems to violate the first, is not shading, but pointillism, another technique that was used by Byzantine mosaicists. The technique was used to achieve a graduated shading (plate 14); but it is not, any more than anamorphosis, an intrinsically naturalistic technique. In the simplest case, a pointillist painter might depict a green lawn by means of a large number of tiny dabs of blue and yellow. This is certainly a technique of which Plato would have disapproved. 'Owing to errors of vision about colours,' he might have said, 'things of certain colours appear to be of other colours, when viewed from far. And pointillism, in its exploitation of this weakness of our nature falls nothing short of witchcraft . . .'

At a distance, the part of the canvas which depicts the lawn appears to be an evenly coloured green surface. But when we look more closely, we can see that its appearance from a distance was misleading. What about the lawn? From a distance, it seems to be green. Should we say: when we look more closely, it becomes apparent that the lawn is really blue and yellow? Of course not! On the contrary, it is necessary to misperceive the colour of the part of the canvas which depicts the lawn in order to perceive correctly the colour of the lawn: and when we are too close to the painting, we can no longer see what it depicts; the lawn becomes invisible.

If this argument is correct, then it follows that neither perspective diminution nor anamorphosis violates Plato's first requirement of likeness-making, and neither shading nor pointillism violates his second requirement. (Note that perspective diminution and anamorphosis are not alternatives: the use of one of these techniques does not preclude the simultaneous use of the other; and the same goes for shading and pointillism.) These requirements were: first, that a likeness must conform to the proportions of the original in all three dimensions; and second, that it must give the proper colour to each part. Perspective diminution and shading, far from violating these requirements, actually allow them to be satisfied, since they provide the painter with the means to show, for example, the (non-planar) spatial relations of the parts of a building, or the plasticity of a face. Shading collaborates well with foreshortening, as in the depiction of a shield (plate 15), which, not least because of its simple shape, was one of the first objects to be depicted by means of either technique.

The techniques that exploit tendencies to particular kinds of misperception are not those whose invention marked the inception of naturalism, that is, perspective diminution and shading, but anamorphosis and pointillism; and these techniques, far from belonging particularly in the repertoire of naturalistic artists, were most profitably used by tenth-and eleventh-century mosaicists. However, anamorphosis and pointillism, whilst they may thus be said to exploit weaknesses of our nature, nevertheless do not cause us, for example, to misperceive the colour of a depicted lawn; and hence their use does not require that such a part of a depicted scene does not have the colour of the original. A good pointillist ensures precisely that it does. Thus, even in the case of those pictorial techniques which do exploit weaknesses of our nature, such as a painting or a sculpture designed to be seen from an eccentric point of view, the complaint that 'artists, leaving the truth to take care of itself, give their figures, not the real proportions, but those that look right [καλάς]' is confused. The proportions of a depicted figure are ascertained by inspection, not by measurement. If a sculpture is designed to be seen from an eccentric point of view then the proportions of the sculpted figure will very likely be misperceived if the sculpture is viewed from straight ahead, just as the colour of a pointillist's lawn may be misperceived if his painting is not viewed from a sufficient distance.

This point is nicely illustrated by a (presumably fantastic) story recorded by Tzetzes (Overbeck, 1868, § 772): The Athenians commissioned two statues of Athena, one by Phidias, the other by Alkamenes, which were to be placed on high columns. Phidias 'a student of vision, a geometrician and a wise man' knew that 'what is at a height seems smallest', and therefore exaggerated the facial features of his statue. Because of this, he was almost stoned. But when the statues were in place, his skill became apparent, and it was Alkamenes who was laughed at.

It is clear why Plato's example of *phantastikē* is a sculpture. When the Stranger divides the art of image-making into two kinds, it has been agreed that the sophist is an imitator of things (μιμητὴς ὢν τῶν ὄντων) (235a): the purpose of the division is to show that the things that the sophist imitates are mere appearances. The difference between the apparent and the actual proportions of a statue serves as a perspicuous example of the gap between appearance and reality; in particular, because this gap is best exposed by measurement.[5] However, this has nothing to do with the fact that the statue is an imitation, i.e. a figurative work of art: certain of the subtleties of curvature and other refinements introduced into the design of the Parthenon would have served just as well. The thickening of the corner columns, for example, was designed to compensate for the appearance of thinness that they would otherwise have had, as a result

[5] 'Have not measuring and numbering and weighing,' asks Socrates, 'proved to be most gracious aids to prevent the domination in our soul of the apparently greater or less or more or heavier, and to give control to that which has reckoned and numbered or even weighed?' (*Rep.*, 602d; cf. *Protagoras*, 356d–e.)

of their brighter background.⁶ The example of *phantastikē* is not simply a sculpture rather than a painting: it is a sculpture *qua* measurable block of stone, and has nothing whatsoever to do with mimetic art.

Plato's distinction between *eikastikē* and *phantastikē* proved to be very flexible and caught on fast. The sculptor Lysippus, whose earliest works Plato may have seen, employed the distinction in the service of a conception of art diametrically opposed to Plato's own, for he was evidently proud to be an exponent of the art of *phantastikē* (Pliny (*NH*, XXXIV, 65) records that Lysippus 'used commonly to say that whereas his predecessors had made men as they really were, he made them as they appeared to be'); and despite the fact that it was utterly confused, the distinction has exercised the profoundest influence on the history and theory of art.

II

Johann Joachim Winckelmann's revolutionary essay *Reflections on the Imitation of Greek Works in Painting and Sculpture* was published in 1755, and his *History of the Art of the Ancients* appeared in 1764, the first modern history of ancient art. Winckelmann did not, of course, share Plato's prejudice against the use of perspective diminution and shading; neither did he regard the reproduction of the appearance of

---

⁶ According to some writers, another example is the inward inclination of the corner columns, which was supposedly designed to avoid the appearance of an outward slant that perfectly upright corner columns would have had as a result of their tapering. A.W. Lawrence writes that this was 'a most persistent "refinement", used long after the majority of those invented in the fifth century had been discarded. It became such a matter of course that Cicero could repeat, without a word of explanation even to a Roman audience, the story of how the Governor of Sicily swindled a contractor over the repairs to a temple by testing the columns with a plumb-line and condemning them as crooked.' (Lawrence, 1983, p. 227)

Lawrence suggests that the architects of the Parthenon, which was built between 447 and 438 BC, were influenced by Democritus's and Anaxagoras's investigation of perspective. However, this hypothesis would seem to evince the same confusion between anamorphosis and perspective diminution. Besides, the hypothesis depends upon the traditional dating of Agatharcus' backdrop.

the human form as the mere appearance of the reproduction of the human form. Nevertheless, he was perfectly satisfied with the distinction between *eikastikē* and *phantastikē*. 'The most ancient records teach us,' he wrote, 'that the earliest essays, especially in the drawing of figures, have represented, not the manner in which a man appears to us, but what he is; not a view of his body, but the outline of his shadow.' (Winckelmann, 1881, p. 134)

The reaction against Winckelmann's apotheosis of classical Greek art began soon after the publication of his *History*. Herder's cultural pluralism, and the broader tastes and far broader knowledge of succeeding generations, challenged Winckelmann's exclusive celebration of the classical ideal; and the growing interest in Egyptian art, whose history did not conform to any such pattern, undermined his picture of the evolution of Greek art as an inexorable process of perfection and decay. This picture had masked the lack of any historical explanation of stylistic transformation, and gradually, in the course of the nineteenth century, the explanatory gap opened. Napoleon's invasion of Egypt, the development of archaeology, the metaphysics of Hegel, and the transformation of biological science all played a part in this process; and the explanation of stylistic change became, in the second half of the nineteenth century, the chief goal of art historical research.[7]

The most influential attempt to fill this explanatory gap, in respect of the inception of naturalism, was Emanuel Loewy's *The Rendering of Nature in Early Greek Art*, which was published in 1900. According to Loewy, artists have always sought to 'seize the forms of nature' (1907, p. 24), but it was only gradually that they could overcome the psychological barriers to the reproduction of the retinal image, and thereby 'copy a given aspect of reality' (ibid., p. 17), rather than a 'memory-picture' (*Errinerungsbild*). 'Along with the pictures that reality presents to the eye,' he writes,

there exists another world of images, living or coming into life in our minds alone, which, though indeed suggested by reality, are nevertheless essentially metamorphosed. Every primitive artist,

[7] For the history of the historiography of art in the nineteenth century, v. Kidson, 1984, pp. 401–5; Gombrich, 1969, III and IV; and Podro, 1982, which also contains a bibliography.

when endeavouring to imitate nature, seeks with the spontaneity
of a psychical function to reproduce merely these mental images.
And so it was with the [early, non-naturalistic] Greek artist . . .
Where we are able to follow up an entire development of art,
there we find that its morphological progress is from the
psychical to the physical, i.e. to the image on the retina . . .
(pp. 18 and 33)

Loewy's theory of art has four components: (1) non-naturalistic
artists, such as children and ancient Egyptians, reproduce mental
images, and (2) they do so *faute de mieux*; (3) naturalistic artists, for
example the Greek painters who practised the art of *skiagraphia*,
reproduce their retinal images; (4) in any 'entire development of art',
there is an historical tendency from non-naturalistic art towards
naturalistic art but never from naturalistic art towards non-naturalistic
art.

It should be noted to begin with that Loewy nowhere attempts to
explain why, when men had always vainly striven to 'seize the forms of
nature', the Greeks finally succeeded in the fifth century BC. He
suggests that this achievement was an achievement of self-discipline, a
matter of overcoming a psychological impulse. But he does not address
the question, what enabled the Greeks of the fifth century to master the
innate propensity for non-naturalistic art that they shared with the rest
of humanity? Whatever Loewy achieved, it was not an historical
explanation of the inception of naturalism.

However, the first proposition is intended to provide a psychological
explanation for the quadrifaciality of archaic Greek *kouroi*, and for the
fact that each of the main features of a (non-naturalistic) painted figure
is depicted as if it were projected onto a plane perpendicular to the line
of sight which reveals its most distinctive and, on the whole, its
broadest aspect. (Hence, the various features are depicted as if
projected onto separate planes.) Loewy's explanation depends upon the
notion of a memory-picture. This is a Janus-faced entity – now a
concept, '[a] Platonic Idea . . . clear of everything individual or
accidental' (p. 10), and now a mental image. These memory-pictures,
supposedly derived by a process of abstraction from sense-impressions,
are mysteriously accumulated and stored in the mind; they are, in a

phrase which echoes Locke, 'assimilated to the common store' (p. 27). Like many writers with scientific pretensions, Loewy identified the sense-impressions with retinal images, or at any rate their immediate reflection in consciousness.[8]

The proposition that archaic Greek *kouroi* and early Greek (and Egyptian) paintings are reproductions of memory-pictures, that is image-like concepts, is deeply confused. First, to possess a concept is not to have mental image of something; it is not to visualize something clearly or vaguely, to see something in one's mind's eye. And the use of a concept is not an exercise of the visual imagination.

Second, concepts do not 'live or come into life in our minds alone', although the possession of a concept is an accomplishment of which only a creature with a mind is capable. Whilst Loewy's phrase is far from lucid, presumably sensations, hallucinations and mental images are the kinds of things that are supposed to 'live in our minds'. But having a concept is not like having a toothache. The ascription of sensations and of linguistic abilities can both be couched in terms of ownership, although neither sensations nor concepts can be numbered among a man's possessions, as can a lease or a freehold: the form of representation, viz. ownership, serves in both cases as a syntactic expedient, rather than signifying a sort of ownership. But it is used quite differently in the two cases. Thus, you and I share a great many concepts, but we cannot share a toothache. I might, with a lot of study, acquire and use Marx's concept of alienation, but I can no more have his angina than his heart-attack. The phrase 'live or come into life in our minds alone', if it serves any purpose, serves to capture these necessary truths about sensations, hallucinations and mental images –

---

[8] In spite of his casual denial of any familiarity with psychologial literature, it is likely that the sources of Loewy's perceptual theory were Wilhelm Wundt and Herman von Hemholtz. Helmhotz's *Popular Scientific Lectures*, including 'On the Relation of Optics to Painting', were published in 1873. Indeed, Helmholtz anticipated this sort of application of perceptual theory to the discussion of naturalism: 'We must look upon [naturalistic] artists,' he claimed, 'as persons whose observation of sensuous impressions [i.e. retinal images or their immediate, unconceptualized reflections in consciousness] is particularly vivid and accurate, and whose memory for these images is particularly true' (1968, p. 140). Elsewhere, he remarks that 'it is well known that one of the greatest difficulties in perspective drawing is to eliminate the influence which one's idea of the true size of seen objects automatically exercises.'

that they are not shared or passed from one person to another. But then concepts cannot be said to 'live or come into life in our minds alone'.

Third, there is no such thing as a picture of a concept. The proposition that a painting of a certain sort depicts a concept is simply unintelligible, because only what can be described in terms that would serve as the description of something visible can be depicted. (This is simply a corollary of the necessary truth that the subject of a painting is determined by looking at it.) Thus, a smell or a sound cannot be depicted, except by means of a sort of pictorial synaesthetic metaphor (plate 16). Of course, what is depicted need not be included in the range of visibilia. For example, the woodblock print by Koryusai reproduced here (plate 17) depicts a courtesan's day-dream, although dreams and mental images are not visible: they cannot be illuminated or occluded, and they are not reflected in mirrors or captured on photographic plates. But concepts are neither visible nor depictible. A picture of a man that is painted in a style which excludes the depiction of his blemishes or idiosyncrasies is not therefore a picture of the concept of a man. A man depicted in an Egyptian painting has arms and legs: the concept of a man does not.

Fourth and finally, whilst figure 21 evidently depicts a mental image, that is it depicts what the courtesan's mental image was of, it is absurd to suggest that every Egyptian painting and every child's drawing does so. Must we say, for example, that a picture of Polyphemus painted around 660 BC (plate 18), depicts a mental image of the Cyclops, whereas a picture painted two hundred and fifty years later (plate 19) depicts the Cyclops himself, or a retinal image of him? And does figure 6 depict a mental image of the reproduction of a mental image, whatever that may be?

Loewy's first proposition was that non-naturalistic artists, such as children and ancient Egyptians, reproduce memory-pictures. This, Loewy believed, explained why *kouroi* are quadrifacial, and why early Greek and Egyptian figure-painting is distinctively schematic in design. But the proposition is strictly unintelligible, and incorporates a similarly unintelligible philosophical psychology. So, why did Loewy imagine that the arcane stuff of nineteenth-century psychology would allow him to explain these facts about ancient art?

The answer to this question is that it was the key to a sort of intellectual alchemy: by means of it, an ancient analogy (see for

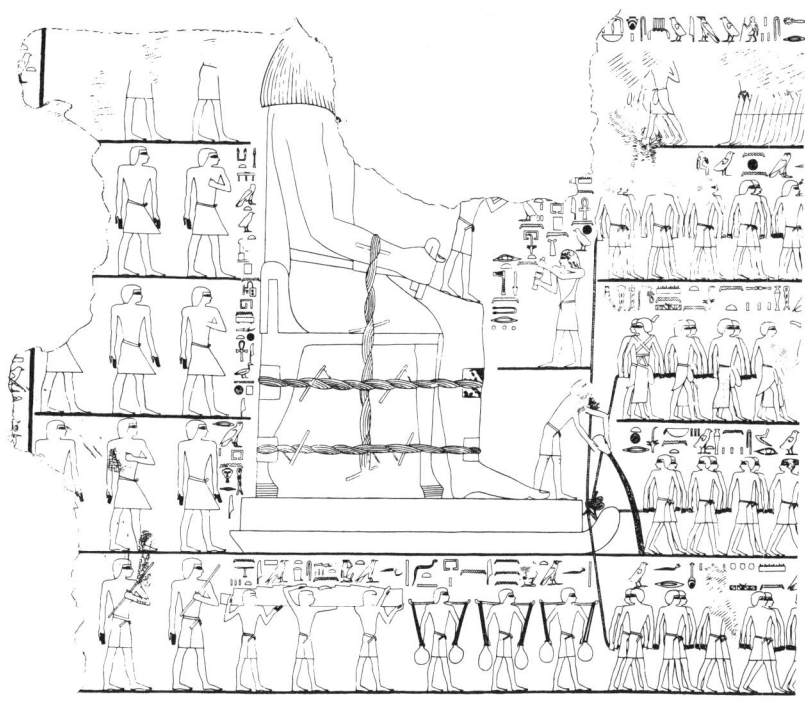

FIGURE 6 Transporting a colossal statue: Middle Kingdom.

example the passage from Plato's *Statesman* reproduced above, p. 88)
was transmuted into an explanatory hypothesis. Stated directly, the
analogy is harmless but not particularly illuminating: Egyptian figures
can be analyzed into a conjunction of discrete and characteristic
elements, and *kouroi* can be analyzed into a conjunction of discrete
views, rather as the concept of a man, a horse or a tree can, by means of
a definition, by analyzed into a conjunction of characteristic features. It
is arguable that Loewy's use of the analogy betrays a confusedly narrow
conception of definition (v. Baker and Hacker, 1980, pp. 77f), as
well as a misconceived philosophical psychology. Be that as it may, the
first proposition – that non-naturalistic artists reproduce memory-
pictures – does not explain the quadrifaciality of *kouroi* or the
distinctively schematic appearance of early Greek and Egyptian figure-

painting;[9] it is simply a metaphorical reiteration, decked out in the fashionable paraphernalia of nineteenth-century philosophical psychology, of the fact that *kouroi* are quadrifacial, and the fact that early Greek and Egyptian figures are distinctively schematic in design.

Nevertheless, it was the failure of historical imagination evinced by Loewy's second proposition, that non-naturalistic artists reproduce psychical images *faute de mieux*, rather than the conceptual confusion evinced by the first, that drew fire.[10] Heinrich Schäfer, whose *Principles of Egyptian Art* was first published in 1919, accepted without cavil Loewy's psychological distinction between naturalistic and non-naturalistic art: 'The rendering of a pre-Greek does not correspond to a visual impression . . . but to a mental image . . . The work of art embodies this image.'[11] (Schäfer, 1974, p. 91) In contrast, the classical Greek artist employed a method that 'reproduces visual impressions faithfully, basing itself on the visual image built into the structure of the human eye.' (p. 269) But he explicitly rejected Loewy's second proposition: 'It is still believed', he wrote, 'that drawing with foreshortening is a stage of development that is reached everywhere by every gifted person or people. If it is not reached, the person, it is said, cannot be gifted, or, as with the Egyptian people, must be held back by some constraint . . . This attitude is wrong.'

---

[9] Wittkower attributes the quadrifaciality of *kouroi* to the draughtsmanlike approach of archaic sculptors to the four sides of the block; and this is surely right. 'The silhouettes of [archaic *kouroi*]', he writes, 'clearly disclose the original block form. In front of the finished piece (plate 20) one feels doubly sure that, while working on the front, the back, and the sides, the sculptor must always have taken his bearings from the early outline drawings: as he faced each side of his figures he thought in draughtsmanlike terms . . . As a result of this, the finished figure must have four distinct views' (Wittkower, 1979, p. 18). However, Wittkower is wrong to attribute the change in method to the invention of harder alloys that permitted tools to be used at an angle to the surface of the stone, for the Greeks invented the claw chisel in the first half of the sixth century. Rather, it was probably due to the use of modelling, whether for casting or as a model for carving.

[10] The third proposition, that naturalistic artists reproduce their retinal images, was discussed in the last chapter. The fourth proposition resists discussion, since it is unclear what is meant by 'an entire development of art'; but it seems that the proposition is false on any definition of the phrase that is not, so to speak, purpose-built.

[11] Schäfer describes Egyptian art as 'image-based' (*vorstellig*) and also as 'based on frontal images' (*geradvorstellig*). The latter word was his own coinage.

(p. 269) '[Loewy] could not avoid observing that memory excludes certain types of view, in fact foreshortened ones, but did not ask himself why this should be. So in the end he never solved the problem, indeed never posed the final question.' (p. 89)

In other words, Schäfer contended, against Loewy, that the distinctive character of Egyptian art was the result of a deliberate choice, rather than the failure to govern a psychological impulse. When it comes to identifying the reason for this choice – and answering 'the final question' – Schäfer draws directly on Plato:

The basic motive for avoiding foreshortening [was] an attempt to get around the contradiction between perspective sense data and 'objective' reality; or rather the experience of this contradiction is the reason why perception and even conscious observation of the oblique views and foreshortenings of perspective have no effect on pre-Greek draughtsmen . . . The user of the 'pre-Greek' method . . . aims to show things objectively as they are, or as they live in his imagination . . . (p. 89)

Loewy had transformed the analogy between definition and non-naturalistic depiction into a psychological explanation of the distinctive characteristics of non-naturalistic art: Schäfer's theoretical achievement was a synthesis of this deeply confused psychology of art and Plato's spurious distinction between *eikastikē* and *phantastikē*.

Loewy and Schäfer were heirs to an historiographical tradition, fostered by Wundt and exemplified by Karl Lamprecht, which consciously sought to distinguish stages of cultural evolution in terms of psychological criteria. But the appeal of Schäfer's synthesis of Loewy's psychological system and Plato's defence of traditional art has far outlived that sort of history: sometimes altered in one significant particular, Schäfer's theory is now promulgated by the mainstream of art historians and psychologists interested in the historical explanation of the inception of naturalism.

The alteration, towards which Schäfer was already inclined,[12] first

---

[12] Schäfer was not entirely happy with stigmatization of naturalism implicit in Plato's contrast between *eikastikē*, the reproduction of reality, and *phantastikē*, the reproduction of appearance. Thus, he denies that the invention of perspective signified, 'as Plato would have it, a descent into deceptive appearances' (Schäfer, 1974,

appears plainly in Erwin's Panofsky's influential article *Die Perspektive als 'Symbolische Form'*, which was published in 1924:

> The exact perspective construction . . . disregards the very great difference between the psychologically determined 'visual image', which brings the visible world to our awareness, and the mechanically determined retinal image painted on our physical eye (for a peculiar 'tendency towards constancy' of our conscious awareness . . . attributes to the things we see a definite size and shape belonging to them as such, and therefore is disposed to ignore either wholly or in part the apparent changes which these sizes and shapes undergo in the retinal image). (Panofsky, 1924, p. 259.)

Panofsky's innovation was to replace Loewy's distinction between the retinal image and the memory-picture with a distinction drawn by means of the apparatus of constancy scaling, which will be familiar to the reader from chapter 3. With or without this modification the theory has held sway ever since.

To sum up: Plato's indignation at the deceitful art that appeals to the basest part of the soul now seems very strange. However, his distinction between *eikastikē* and *phantastikē*, which assigns naturalistic art and traditional art respectively to the categories of Appearance and Reality, has not lost its appeal. The distinction is often couched in

---

p. 272). And yet a few pages earlier he states that 'out of all the peoples in the world the Greeks are the only ones . . . to represent the world of appearances which our eye presents to us multifariously distorted' (p. 269). This ambivalence derives from Schäfer's failure to think critically about the psychological system that he employed. Sometimes the Egyptian painter is conceived as selecting from amongst his visual impressions those that he wishes to reproduce: 'Any draughtsman's senses give him a host of perceptions of different objects, and of one and the same object. The 'pre-Greek' rejects from these the ones with a perspective character . . .' (p. 89) At other times he is conceived as reproducing mental images, that is visual impressions which have been 'processed' to correct their misleading characteristics: '[Experience teaches us] to correct the appearance of perspective, or to remove it because it is an illusion which distorts things . . . The brain of a pre-Greek man performs the correction so often and with such quiet confidence that the contradiction will only occasionally strike him and force him to make a decision.' (p. 88) The second picture, which anticipates Panofsky's modification, sits easily with the stigmatization of perspective diminution, but the first does not.

terms of psychological rather than metaphysical categories, that is in terms of 'how things strike us visually' and 'how we know them to be'. Great mistakes are adaptable: just how adaptable is shown by the examples collected in the appendix to this chapter.

III

Recent attempts at the historical explanation of the inception of naturalism have not been thwarted by innaccurate chronology, or by the lack of surviving works of art (although next to no Greek painting has survived from the fifth century), or by the lack of any other historical data, but by their authors' unquestioning acceptance of Plato's distinction between *eikastikē* and *phantastikē*, and by the confusions inherent in the psychological system into which this distinction was fitted. The grip exerted by Plato and mediated by the arcane apparatus of nineteenth-century philosophical psychology has ensured that the discussion of the inception of naturalism has never gone beyond the futile and confused reiteration of the problem. There is as yet nothing that can be counted as a candidate for a solution.

The final section of this chapter is intended as a prolegomenon to the historical explanation of the inception of naturalism. A coherent description of the achievement of the Greek artists working during the extraordinary period following the Persian Wars, a description that is contaminated neither by Platonic metaphysics nor by nineteenth-century philosophical psychology, by itself explains nothing. Nor does it provide any means of assessing the correctness of putative explanations of the phenomena described. But it should make it more difficult to propose pseudo-explanations of the sort already examined.

I think it is possible to arrive at a clear conception of the difference between relatively non-naturalistic and relatively naturalistic modes of depiction by considering a remark that Loewy makes about early Greek painted pottery. Writing about the vases of the Geometric Period depicting the *prothesis*, the lying-in-state of the dead, he asks:

Who will be surprised by the dead men on these vases, lying rigidly on their sides for the sake of preserving full visibility in the sense of the mental image, when a considerably later period of painting, in spite of what the situation required, draws the companions of Ulysses hanging down, not directly under the rams, but all on one side? (Loewy, 1907, pp. 22–3)

Loewy's remark is confused: the drawing and painting, which I have reproduced as figure 7 and plate 21, do not depict a man hanging all on one side of the ram, or a man hanging directly under the ram, for the depicted scene is almost entirely lacking in non-planar spatial relations. It makes perfect sense to ask whether the man is above or beneath the ram; but it does not make sense to ask which lies further from the viewer. To be sure, the figure of the man overlaps the figure of the ram, but overlapping does not in this case depict occlusion (see below, p. 106), as the spatial unintelligibility of the adjacent figure confirms.

Loewy's remark, that the man is hanging 'all on one side', is therefore not false, as it would probably be of an eighteenth-century French depiction of the same subject, but senseless because the style in which the scene is depicted precludes the coherence of the question to which it is an answer. Modes of depiction differ in what can and what

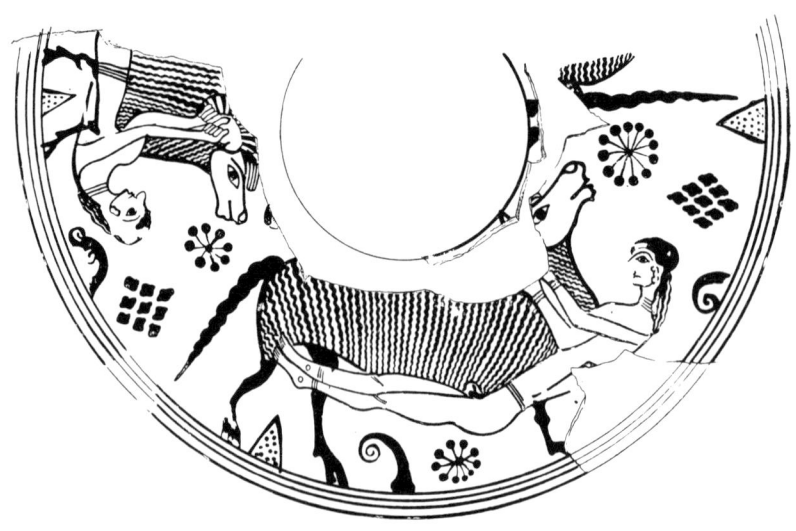

FIGURE 7 Loewy: Drawing from the Ram Jug (plate 21).

cannot be depicted, and hence what can and cannot be asked about the scene depicted. *The development of naturalism was the gradual enlargement of the range of questions that could coherently be asked about a depicted scene.*[13]

Loewy's mistake was to answer a question beyond the range appropriate to the style in which the picture was painted, one that makes no more sense than the question of what mental processes led Adam to accept the forbidden fruit. It is quite commonly observed that in plastic as in literary art we cannot always ask about the mental life of the actors. Gombrich, for example (1977, p. 114), comments that a question of this sort 'might have struck an Egyptian as it would strike us if someone inquired the age or mood of the king on the chessboard.' My point is simply that the same goes for several other sorts of question that we are accustomed to ask about early Greek, Assyrian, Egyptian and other non-naturalistic pictures, in particular, questions about the orientation of and spatial relations between different parts of a depicted scene. In order to depict non-planar spatial relations it is necessary to depict occlusion properties, as the argument of the last chapter shows. But whilst Egyptian, Assyrian and early Greek artists did depict the simplest of these, the partial occlusion of one feature of the scene by another, they did not depict relative occlusion size or occlusion shape. (For the minor exceptions to this generalization, v. Schäfer, 1974, 5.1, and Iversen, 1975, p. 31.)

Partial occlusion – in other words, the partial invisibility of one feature as a result of its spatial relation to another – is depicted by the partial depiction of the occluded feature: the part of the picture plane where the rest of the feature would normally be depicted depicts instead the part of the nearer feature that occludes it. Although strictly speaking a picture of a man carrying a spear or a length of rope will depict the partial occlusion of the rope by the man's hand (plate 22), it is best to reserve the concept for those cases where the features of the depicted scene are not physically connected, and hence where one object is brought into a purely spatial relation with another, rather than

---

[13] The same is true of naturalistic drama. As Arthur Miller wrote, 'it is the nature of the questions asked and answered, rather than the language used – whether verse, ordinary slang, or colorless prose – that determines whether the style is realistic or non-realistic.' (1967, p. 5)

being, for example, grasped, used or thrown. Egyptian pictures of overlapping figures, humans or animals, are obvious examples of the depiction of partial occlusion (plate 4).

Assyrian reliefs include many overlapping figures, although overlapping is not invariably a means of depicting occlusion: it may simply permit the artist to pack the figures more closely, without carrying any implication about the spatial relations between them. A relief from Kuyunjik depicting the capture of an Elamite city (plate 23), for example, shows the women and children of Madaktu leaving the city, preceded by a band of musicians. The four harps shown here (and two others) are all depicted in full, but it would be a mistake to infer that each harpist is closer to the picture plane than the figure to the left which is partially occluded by the harp. The purpose of the arrangement is simply to allow the harps to be shown in full, without thinning the crowd. Similarly, in a scene from the Bayeux tapestry (plate 24) the overlapping of the horses was not intended to depict the spatial relations between them: it simply meant that the horses could be crowded more closely than otherwise.

Egyptian painters did depict simple non-planar spatial relations: for example, a row of figures along a line orthogonal to the picture plane. But they did not depict relative occlusion size or occlusion shape; they did not distinguish, except during the reign of King Amenophis IV (Akhenaten), between open right hands and open left hands or between right feet and left feet; and they did not depict the direction of illumination, or the quality of illumination, i.e. whether it was such as to cast clear shadows.

Egyptian painters did not employ the technique of shading, and they did not depict cast shadows, but not because they did not possess the concept of a shadow, or because the mental image of a man shows him diffusely illuminated from the front. Egyptian painters did not possess the technique of shading, and it is therefore senseless to ask the direction of the illumination of a depicted scene: the question simply does not arise. And whereas the most dazzling of Monet's paintings of Rouen evidently depicts the cathedral at noon, it would be senseless to ask the time of day at which Nebamun hunts birds and spears fish. (And it would be as fanciful to argue that this is because the sun does not rise and set in the afterlife as it would be to ague that those who enjoy an afterlife do so with two left feet.)

The depiction of spatial relations by Egyptian painters is a more complex problem. However, the limits upon the depiction of non-planar spatial relations may be summarized as follows: there are cases where the question of the relative distance from the spectator of two depicted figures is inappropriate, even though the figures overlap, but unless the figures overlap they cannot stand in a non-planar spatial relation to each other. It is this, and not the orientation of mental images of heads, or the alleged fact that 'the head was most easily seen in profile' (Gombrich, 1972, p. 35), that explains the ubiquity of the profile in Egyptian, Assyrian and early Greek painting and relief carving, for if human figures are engaged an activity, whether it is fighting or dancing or reaping or catching an antelope, which takes place as it were along a corridor perpendicular to the spectator's line of sight, then they can but face to his left or to his right. The logic of a narrative art constrained by the lack of non-planar spatial relations, and not the ungovernable impulse to reproduce a psychic image, to 'represent the subject as it was known to exist in the mind's eye' (Aldred, 1980, p. 30), explains the ubiquity of the profile in early Near Eastern art.[14]

The depiction of the profile became most deeply entrenched in Egyptian art, probably because the convention was reinforced by the use of the profile for the hieroglyph ' 𓁀 ' meaning 'head', as opposed to ' 𓁷 ' which meant 'face'.[15] As a result, even devotional images,

---

[14] By 'narrative art' I do not only mean art that depicts myth, legend or history: I mean the depiction of human activities, as opposed to the simple depiction of the human form, e.g. as part of a decorative scheme or the devotional purposes.

The Bayeux Tapestry illustrates the contrast clearly. There are approximately five hundred and fifty heads depicted in the surviving part of the tapestry, exluding the borders. Of these, three are definitely shown in full face. There are a few borderline cases, e.g. King Edward enthroned, and seventy to eighty three-quarter views. The three figures clearly shown in full face are King Harold and Archbishop Stigand, beneath the inscription, 'Here Harold, King of England sits enthroned', and Bishop Odo, who may have had the tapestry made, beneath the inscription, 'And here the Bishop blesses the food and wine'. Roughly the last quarter of the tapestry depicts the battle. Here every one of the one hundred and forty odd heads is in profile, as are the many corpses and archers in the lower border. Every severed head, and there are plenty of them, is shown in profile! (See plates 25, 26 and 27.)

[15] The unique proximity of writing and depiction in ancient Egypt is dramatically illustrated by the inscriptions on statues of the Archaic Period and the Old Kingdom. These inscriptions were usually confined to the owner's title and name, but the

which generally answer the gaze of the spectator, showed the figures of gods, and the figures of dead men on false doors (plate 28), in profile. More normal are the Assyrian reliefs of baked clay which replaced the cult statue in small shrines, and show the gods in frontal view.

Devotional images generally do not depict actors in a narrative, and the importance of the profile to a narrative art lacking non-planar spatial relations will be appreciated if one considers the exceptions to this generalization, the Byzantine images of the stories of the Gospels. Byzantine artists were faced with the problem of depicting narrative scenes involving actors virtually all of whom had to be depicted frontally. The depiction of the annunciation was perhaps the most difficult case, since it is a story of speech. The only solution that was entirely satisfactory – it was ingenious, as it had to be – was to warp the picture plane, so that the angel and the Virgin face each other across a corner (plate 29).

Consider again the Third Dynasty relief of Hesire (plate 28). In such a case it is a mistake to regard the depicted figure as facing the spectator's right, just as it is a mistake to suppose that he has two left feet: the question of the direction of his gaze is another that is ruled out, but not in this case by the lack of a pictorial technique.[16] It is ruled out because the use of the profile was determined by the convention that a head was painted, carved or incised *thus*. This is not an iconographic convention: it would be absurd to argue that because the colour of the Virgin's cloak is determined by convention, it is a mistake to suppose that it has a deter.ninate colour. It is a technical convention – originally derived from the exigencies of narrative art, where it served precisely to guarantee the direction of the gaze of a depicted figure – more akin to the conventional use of a gold ground on an altarpiece or to the technical conventions of oriental ink-painting than to any iconographic convention. The development of naturalism, the enlargement of the range of question that could coherently be asked about a depicted scene,

determinative which would normally follow the phonetic hieroglyphs when a name was written or inscribed was omitted on the base of the statue. The statue itself functioned as a determinative. (V. Fischer, 1978, pp. 3–4.)

[16] Schäfer correctly describes this sort of relief as 'neutral as to direction' (1974, p. 218); but he is wrong to conclude that 'the description of the dead man as standing in the door [i.e. facing out] renders accurately the image in the artist's mind.' (Ibid.)

was thus the result both of the invention of specific pictorial techniques and of the rejection or transformation of traditional methods of depiction. (These two kinds of achievement were not completely independent, as the example of the profile shows.) Some of these, for example the customary method for depicting an eye, were simply traditional workshop techniques; others were explicitly governed by convention, such as those that determined the proportions of a depicted human figure.

The art of ancient Egypt was preeminent in taking accord with customary practice and convention as its standard of success, and nowhere is this more apparent than in the method it employed to determine the proportions of a depicted human figure. Thus the tomb stela of the sculptor Iritisen, who lived in the Middle Kingdom, records a hierarchy of rule-governed activities that Iritisen had practised, and includes his expertise in the employment of the canon of proportions after his religious and metrological skills, but first amongst his pictorial ones: 'I am' it reads, 'an expert craftsman, renowned for my knowledge. I know the methods of pouring [offerings?], and of weighing according to standard weights; the methods of construction that give each part [of the body] its proper place; I know how to reproduce the qualities of statues of men, and the pose of statues of women . . .' In fact, the very nature of the Egyptian canon, its intimate relation to the Egyptian system for the measurement of length,[17] made this inevitable.

The Egyptian system for the measurement of length, like every other system until the decimal, was anthropometric. Its units corresponded to parts of the human body, and the relations between the units were approximately determined by the normal metrical relations between these parts of the body. Thus, in the original system, the Small Cubit corresponded to the distance between the elbow and the tip of the thumb, and was divided into six palms; and the palm was divided into four digits. Four palms made a Two-Thirds Measure, which corresponded to the distance from elbow to shoulder. Four cubits made a fathom, which corresponded to the distance from thumb to thumb with arms outstretched and also to the height of a standing man.

[17] This was properly understood for the first time by Eric Iversen. For a detailed discussion of the Egyptian canon, v. Iversen, 1975.

The Egyptian canon basically consisted of the proportions between the parts of the body contained in the metrological system. Thus the arm of a depicted figure was deemed to be correctly proportioned if the distance between the shoulder and the elbow was five times the distance across the palm, the distance from the hairline to the base of a male figure was twenty-four times the distance across the palm, and so forth. Obviously, the use of this system ensured that a depicted human figure looked, in respect of proportion, as a human figure should; but it would be a mistake to regard the canon as a recipe for depicting human figures that look well-proportioned. A good cake is one that tastes good, and a good recipe is one that tends to produce delicious cakes. By contrast, a depicted figure, whether it was painted, sculpted or carved, was held to be properly constructed if and only if it was constructed in accordance with the set of mathematical relations that the canon comprised. The canon was adopted, presumably, because its use guaranteed that depicted figures were (visibly) well-proportioned; but once it was accorded a normative role in the production of images, 'well-proportioned', in respect of depicted figures, simply meant 'in accordance with the canon'.[18]

The orthodox view is that naturalistic artists represent their retinal images or their visual impressions, whereas non-naturalistic artists represent concepts or the psychological entities that result from the operations of the constancy mechanism or simply what they know to exist. This view has been tried and found wanting; and so has its ancestor, Plato's thesis that naturalistic artists represent appearance rather than reality. The difference between relatively non-naturalistic and relatively naturalistic modes of depiction does not lie in the kinds of thing represented. Non-naturalistic and naturalistic artists alike represent men and gods, the works of nature and the works of man. The difference is this: by the invention of specific pictorial devices, and

[18] The Polyclitan canon was quite differently conceived. It seems that Polyclitus was deeply influenced by Pythagoreanism, and may have regarded his *Canon* as revealing the mathematical-cum-mystical basis of human proportions, that is as analogous to the Pythagorean account of musical intervals. If so, then Panofsky is wrong to describe the purpose of the Polyclitan canon as 'exclusively to ascertain the "objective" proportions of the normal human being' (Panofsky, 1970, p. 92).

The subsequent change in the conception of the canon is attested by Lysippus's remark, quoted above, p. 94. See also p. 84, n. 1.

by the rejection of transformation of traditional and often explicitly regulated techniques for the production of images, a relatively naturalistic mode of depiction admits a larger range of questions and answers about a depicted scene, one that approximates more closely to the range of questions about the visible environment that can be answered on the basis of visual observation.

I am not qualified to address confidently or in detail the question, why the revolutionary developments in Greek art occurred when they did. However, the actual nature of these developments having been established, there is one feature of their historical context that seems likely to have been related to them. This is the antithesis between *nomos* (law, convention or custom), and *phusis* (nature), which, in the course of the fifth century, came to occupy a central place in philosophical discourse. The antithesis has been extensively discussed, notably by Heinemann, Dodds and Guthrie, but it has not, to my knowledge, been connected with the inception of naturalism.

Rapid legislative change, the emergence of a sort of comparative anthropology, the sense of power that followed the Persian wars and the growth of democracy at Athens have all been adduced as contributory causes of the critical attitude towards tradition which developed in the middle of the fifth century. At any rate, the authority of *nomos* was eroded and, as Dodds writes,

> against the old conception of law, thus stripped of its prestige, it was inevitable that men should set up the new conception of human nature, that they should contrast *nomos* as the variable with *phusis* as the constant. The antithesis was perhaps first made explicit in the special field of medicine: are health and sickness determined mainly by a man's *phusis*, his 'constitution' as we say, or mainly by his *nomos*, i.e. his customary regime of diet, exercise, and so forth? But very soon the problem assumed an ampler scope. When law and human nature conflict, which ought we to follow? Is the social restraint which law imposes on nature a good or a bad thing? For the Sophists that was the grand question. (Dodds, 1973, p. 99)

In fact the problem assumed such a broad scope, serving as a focus for disagreement and stimulating debate in politics, religion and anthropology as well as philosophy, that it is reasonable to suppose that the aims, achievements and principles of the pictorial arts were also analysed and assessed in terms of the antithesis between *nomos* and *phusis*.[19] If so, it is tempting to associate the inception of naturalism – the development of a mode of depiction less constrained by customary practice and convention and more akin, in what may be called its pictorial modality,[20] to the visible world – with this debate.

It seems likely that the antithesis between *nomos* and *phusis* exercised as great an influence on the pictorial arts as on other forms of cultural expression, and that the development of naturalistic techniques was stimulated by this influence. If this analysis is correct, it sheds some light on Plato's analogy between the Sophist and the *skiagraphos*, for they were indeed alike, not in practising deceit, but rather in the challenge to the authority of tradition that they both represented.[21] The great painters of the later fifth century were, like the Sophists, attacked as subversives and defended as liberals. This is not simply because they were innovative painters. Polygnotus and Polyclitus effected no less radical transformations of their artisitic media. It is because they were manifestly, perhaps even avowedly, part of the political and philosophical trend that we associate with the Sophistic movement. Guthrie (1971, p. 48) writes of the Sophists that:

> All alike believed in the antithesis between nature and convention. They might differ in their estimate of the relative value of each, but none of them would hold that human laws, customs and religious beliefs were unshakeable because rooted in an unchanging natural order. These beliefs – or lack of beliefs – were shared by others who were not professional Sophists but came under their influence: Thucydides the historian, Euripides the tragic poet, Critias the aristocrat who also wrote dramas but was one of the most violent of the Thirty Tyrants of 404 BC.

---

[19] There is a trace of the *nomos–phusis* controversy in respect of the pictorial arts in Plato's *Cratylus* [430b–c].

[20] By the phrase 'pictorial modality' I mean the range of questions about a depicted scene that it is possible (i.e. intelligible) to ask and answer on the basis of visual observation.

[21] Hence Plato's approval of the supposedly immutable standards that he believed had governed Egyptian art for ten thousand years (*Laws*, 656d–657a).

To this list I would add the names of the great masters of *skiagraphia*: Agatharchus of Samos, Apollodorus and Zeuxis.

Plato's repugnance towards naturalistic art did not simply reflect an aesthetic idiosyncrasy; his deprecation of it was not simply a spurious philosophical justification for this peculiar prejudice; and his analogy between the Sophists and the painters and sculptors responsible for the inception of naturalism was not without foundation. His antagonism towards them had, as he claimed, a common ground, but this was not the metaphysical ground that he himself alleged.

Appendix

The quotations that comprise this appendix illustrate the influence of Plato's distinction between *eikastikē* and *phantastikē*. The distinction is now generally couched in terms of psychological rather than metaphysical categories, but its power is undiminished. Egyptian art *versus* Greek art, non-perspective painting *versus* perspective painting, neolithic drawing *versus* paleolithic drawing, children's drawing *versus* adult drawing, and even sculpture *versus* painting are distinguished by reference to it.

> Egyptian art . . . displays the same approach to representation which is common to all other ancient peoples before Greek times. All pre-Greek peoples give us a kind of diagram of a thing as man knew it to be, not as it appears to the eye under transitory circumstances. (Smith, 1981, p. 15).

> In seeking to represent three-dimensional objects on a plane surface . . . the Egyptian avoided the perspectival solution of the problem which alone of the nations of antiquity, the Greeks ultimately reached by the fifth century BC. Their vision of the natural world . . . would have seemed to the ancient Egyptian as presumptuous, and concerned only with illusion, a mere distortion of reality. The Egyptian was concerned not with presenting an evanescent personal impression, caught in an instant, but with what he regarded as eternal verities . . .
>
> His non-perspectival vision placed the artist in harmony with a world that he knew to exist. His perception of the forms of nature was derived from a fusion of several aspects recollected in

the tranquillity of his mind and not captured as an instant revelation to the seeing eye. (Aldred, 1980, p. 15).

Egyptian art is not based on what the artist could see at a given moment, but rather on what he knew belonged to a person or a scene. (Gombrich, 1972, p. 36)[1]

[The Greeks] had to overcome . . . the psychological pull toward the distinctive 'conceptual' image that had dominated representation heretofore and that we all have to counteract when we learn the skills of mimesis. (Gombrich, 1977, p. 119)

When an artist employs geometrical perspective he does not draw what he sees – he represents his retinal image. As we know, these are very different, for what is seen is affected by constancy scaling . . . We begin to see why it took so long for perspective to be adopted by painters. In an important sense perspective representations of three dimensions are wrong, for they do not depict the world as it is seen but rather the (idealized) images on the retina. (Gregory, 1977, pp. 174–6)

The peculiar thing about the naturalistic drawings of the Old Stone Age is . . . that they give the visual impression in such a direct, unmixed form, free from all intellectual trimmings or restrictions, that we have to wait until modern impressionism to find any parallels in later art. By the time of the New Stone Age . . . the directness of sensations had been replaced to some

---

[1] Gombrich acknowledges that Loewy's theory fails to explain why the inception of naturalism occurred when it did, but his own attempt to answer this question is no more successful. He suggests that Greek narrative, as we know it from Homer, had a special character which 'set up a chain reaction which transformed the methods of representing the human body – and indeed more than that' (Gombrich, 1977, p. 110).

The idea of a 'chain-reaction', responsible for a revolutionary transformation of art that occurred more than two centuries after it was set in motion, is simply useless as an historiographical tool. But then all that remains of Gombrich's putative explanation is a crude distinction between two kinds of narrative that is obviously contrived to correspond to the spurious distinction between 'conceptual' and 'visual' art: on the one hand there is Homeric narrative, whose special character consists in the fact that 'the poet is . . . an eye-witness' (ibid.); and on the other hand there is a narrative that is ' "conceptual", intent on [an] almost pictographic clarity of form' (pp. 111–12).

extent by the inflexibility of conceptualism. (Hauser, 1962, pp. 2–3)

The major difficulty in drawing . . . is that we are foiled by the achievements of our perceptions, which accord so well with the actual characteristics of objects instead of with the characteristics of the stimulation reaching the eye. This is particularly noticeable in the art of children. If children are asked to copy a table while standing at one end of it, they tend frequently to draw what they perceive: a rectangular surface the far end of which is equal to the near end, with nonconverging sides and length not foreshortened. Plates on the table are likely to be drawn as circles, not ellipses.

A child's drawing of a table is unlikely to be in correct perspective because constancy of size and shape is achieved in perceiving the real table. (Rock, 1984, pp. 106–7)

Our retinas capture an illuminated *visual field* which the act of conscious seeing presents to us as an external *visual world*.

The distinction between these two italicized terms is vital to any scientific analysis of the representational arts. Any relatively full and faithful reproduction of the contents of a visual field is a picture . . . In complete contradistinction, sculpture mimics not the visual *field*, but the visual *world* external to it. (Carpenter, 1960, p. 30)

Bibliography

The following list contains full particulars of books and articles cited in the text or notes. However, ancient works have been omitted because references to the page numbers of particular editions are unhelpful. Unless otherwise stated, passages quoted from Descartes appear in his *Dioptrique*.

Alberti, L. B. 1966: *On Painting*, transl. with intro. and notes by J. R. Spencer. New Haven, Conn.: Yale University Press.

Aldred, C. 1980: *Egyptian Art*. London: Thames and Hudson.

Alhazen (Ibn al Haitham) 1572: *Opticae thesaurus Alhenazi Arabis libri septem.* ed. F. Risner. Basel.

Armstrong, D. M. 1960: *Berkeley's Theory of Vision*. Melbourne: Melbourne University Press.

Austin, J. L. 1962: *Sense and Sensibilia*. Oxford: Oxford University Press.

Baker, G. P. and Hacker, P. M. S. 1980: Wittgenstein: *Understanding and Meaning*. Oxford: Basil Blackwell.

Baxandall, M. 1985: *Patterns of Intention*. New Haven, Conn.: Yale University Press.

Beare, J. I. 1906: *Greek Theories of Elementary Cognition*. Oxford: Oxford University Press.

Berkeley, G. 1975: *Philosophical Works*, intro. and notes by M. R. Ayers. London: Dent.

Blakemore, C. 1977: *Mechanics of the Mind*. Cambridge: Cambridge University Press.

Boltzmann, L. 1974: On the development of the methods of theoretical physics in recent times. In B. McGuiness (ed.), *Ludwig Boltzmann: Theoretical Physics and Philosophical Problems*, transl. by P. Foulkes. Dordrecht, Holland: Reidel.

Boring, E. G. 1942: *Sensation and Perception in the History of Experimental Psychology*. New York: Appleton-Century-Crofts.

Carpenter, R. 1960: *Greek Sculpture*. London: University of Chicago Press.

Crombie, A. C. 1967: The mechanistic hypothesis and the scientific study of vision: Some optical ideas as a background to the invention of the microscope. In S. Bradbury and G. L. E. Turner (eds), *Historical Aspects of Microscopy*. Cambridge: Heffer.

Demus, O. 1948: *Byzantine Mosaic Decoration*. London: Kegan Paul, Trench, Trubner.

Descartes, R. 1953: *Oeuvres et Lettres*, textes présentés par André Bridoux. Paris: Gallimard (Pleiade).

Diels, H. 1897: *Doxographi Graeci*. Berlin: G. Reimer.

Dodds, E. R. 1973: The Sophistic movement and the failure of Greek liberalism. In *The Ancient Concept of Progress and Other Essays*. Oxford: Oxford University Press.

Fischer, H. G. 1978: *Egyptian Studies, II: The Orientation of Hieroglyphs*, part 1, *Reversals*. New York: Metropolitan Museum of Art.

Gaukroger, S. (ed.) 1980: *Descartes: Philosophy, Mathematics and Physics*. Brighton: Harvester.

Gombrich, E. H. 1969: *In Search of Cultural History*. Oxford: Oxford University Press.

Gombrich, E. H. 1972: *The Story of Art*, 12th edn. London: Phaidon.

Gombrich, E. H. 1973: Illusion in art. In E. H. Gombrich and R. L. Gregory (eds), *Illusion in Nature and Art*. London: Duckworth.

Gombrich, E. H. 1977: *Art and Illusion*, 5th edn. Oxford: Phaidon.

Gombrich, E. H. 1982: *The Image and the Eye*. Oxford: Phaidon.

Gregory, R. L. 1964: How the eyes deceive. In *Frontiers of Knowledge*, Modern World Series. London: HMSO.

Gregory, R. L. 1970: *The Intelligent Eye*. London: Weidenfeld and Nicolson.

Gregory, R. L. 1973: The confounded eye. In E. H. Gombrich and R. L. Gregory (eds), *Illusion in Nature and Art*. London: Duckworth.

Gregory, R. L. 1974: *Concepts and Mechanisms of Perception*. London: Duckworth.

Gregory, R. L. 1977: *Eye and Brain*, 3rd edn. London: Weidenfeld and Nicolson.

Grice, H. P. 1961: The causal theory of perception. *Proceedings of the Aristotelian Society*, supp. vol. XXXV.

Guthrie, W. K. C. 1971: *The Sophists*. Cambridge: Cambridge University Press.

Hauser, A. 1962: *The Social History of Art, Vol. 1, From Prehistoric Times to the Middle Ages*. London: Routledge and Kegan Paul.

Held, R. and Richards, W. (eds) 1972: *Perception: Mechanisms and Models*. San Francisco: W. H. Freeman and Co.

Helmholtz, H. von 1968: *Helmholtz on Perception*, ed. R. M. and R. P. Warren. New York: Wiley.

Iverson, E. 1975: *Canon and Proportions in Egyptian Art*. Warminster: Aris and Phillips.

Kenny, A. J. P. 1984: The homunculus fallacy. In *The Legacy of Wittgenstein*. Oxford: Basil Blackwell.

Kepler, J. 1937: *Ad Vitellionem paralipomena quibus astronomiae pars optica traditur*, ed. W. von Dyck and M. Caspar. Munich: C. H. Beck.

Kidson, P. 1984: The figural arts. In M. I. Finley (ed.), *The Legacy of Greece*. Oxford: Oxford University Press.

Krautheimer, R. and Krautheimer-Hess, T. 1956: *Lorenzo Ghiberti*. Princeton, NJ: Princeton University Press.

Lawrence, A. W. 1983: *Greek Architecture*, 4th edn, rev. by R. A. Tomlinson. Harmondsworth: Penguin.

Lindberg, D. C. 1976: *Theories of Vision from Al-Kindi to Kepler*. Chicago: University of Chicago Press.

Locke, J. 1961: *An Essay Concerning Human Understanding*, ed. J. W. Yolton. London: J. M. Dent, 2 vols.

Loewy, E. 1907: *The Rendering of Nature in Early Green Art*, transl. J. Fothergill. London: Duckworth and Co.

Marr, D. 1982: *Vision*. San Francisco: Freeman.

Miller, A. 1967: *Collected Plays*. London: Secker and Warburg.

Overbeck, J. (ed.) 1868: *Die Antiken Schriftquellen zur Geschichte der bildenden Künste bei den Greichen*. Leipzig: W. Engelmann.

Panofsky, E. 1924: Die Perspektive als symbolische Form. In *Vorträge der Bibliothek Warburg*, Nendeln/Liechenstein, pp. 258–330.

Panofsky, E. 1940: *The Codex Huygens and Leonardo da Vinci's Art Theory*. London: The Warburg Institute.

Panofsky, E. 1970: *Meaning in the Visual Arts*. Harmondsworth: Penguin.

Peacocke, C. 1983: *Sense and Content*. Oxford: Oxford University Press.

Pirenne, M. H. 1970: *Optics, Painting and Photography*. Cambridge: Cambridge University Press.

Podro, M. 1982: *The Critical Historians of Art*. New Haven, Conn.: Yale University Press.

Pollitt, J. J. 1974: *The Ancient View of Greek Art*. New Haven and London: Yale University Press.

Quine, W. V. O. 1960: *Word and Object*. Cambridge, Mass.: MIT Press.

Rock, I. 1984: *Perception*. New York: Scientific American Books.

Rosenfeld, I. 1984: Seeing through the brain. *New York Review of Books*, 31 (15).

Sabra, A. I. 1981: *Theories of Light from Descartes to Newton*. Cambridge: Cambridge University Press.

Schäfer, H. 1974: *Principles of Egyptian Art*, ed. E. Brunner-Traut; transl. and ed. J. Baines. Oxford: Oxford University Press.

Scott, J. 1975: *Piranesi*. London: Academy Editions.

Searle, J. 1983: *Intentionality*. Cambridge: Cambridge University Press.

Smith, W. S. 1981: *The Art and Architecture of Ancient Egypt*, 2nd edn, rev. by W. K. Simpson. Harmondsworth: Penguin.

Strawson, P. F. 1974: Causation in perception. In *Freedom and Resentment*. London: Methuen.

Strawson, P. F. 1979: Perception and its objects. In G. F. MacDonald (ed.), *Perception and Identity*. London: Macmillan.

Thouless, R. H. 1931: Phenomenal regression to the real object. *British Journal of Psychology*, 21, 339–59.

Warnock, G. J. 1953: *Berkeley*. Harmondsworth: Penguin.

Weiskrantz, L. 1986: *Blindsight*. Oxford: Oxford University Press.

Weiskrantz, L., Warrington, E. K., Sanders, M. D. and Marshall, J. 1974: Visual capacity in the hemianopic field following a restricted occiptal ablation. *Brain*, 97, 709–28.

Winckelmann, J. J. 1881: *History of Ancient Art*, transl. C. H. Lodge. London: Sampson Low and Co.

Wittgenstein, L. 1958a: *Philosophical Investigations*, 2nd edn, ed. G. E. M. Anscombe and R. Rhees, transl. G. E. M. Anscombe. Oxford: Basil Blackwell.

Wittgenstein, L. 1958b: *The Blue and Brown Books*. Oxford: Basil Blackwell.

Wittgenstein, L. 1968: Wittgenstein's notes for lectures on 'Private Experience' and 'Sense Data', ed. R. Rhees. *Philosophical Review*, 77, pp. 257–320.

Wittgenstein, L. 1971: Remarks on Fraser's *Golden Bough*, transl. A. C. Miles and R. Rhees. *The Human World* (3), 28–41.

Wittgenstein, L. 1976: *Wittgenstein's Lectures on the Foundations of Mathematics*, ed. C. Diamond. Hassocks: Harvester.

Wittgenstein, L. 1980: *Remarks on the Philosophy of Psychology*, vol. 2, ed. G. E. M. Anscombe and G. H. von Wright. Oxford: Basil Blackwell.

Wittkower, R. 1979: *Sculpture*. Harmondsworth: Penguin.

Wollheim, R. 1980: *Art and its Objects*, 2nd edn. Cambridge: Cambridge University Press.

Wollheim, R. 1984: *The Thread of Life*. Cambridge: Cambridge University Press.

Yolton, J. W. 1984: *Perceptual Acquaintance from Descartes to Reid*. Oxford: Basil Blackwell.

Index